Lodz and Getto Litzmannstadt
Promised Land and
Croaking Hole of Europe

ROBERT JAN VAN PELT

Art Gallery of Ontario

FRONT COVER

Henryk Ross, *A view from above the Zigerska Street bridge showing a sentry booth and the Lodz Ghetto gates*, 1940–1941. Print from original 35mm negative. Collection of the Art Gallery of Ontario, gift from the Archive of Modern Conflict, 2007. 2007/2022.276.

TABLE OF CONTENTS

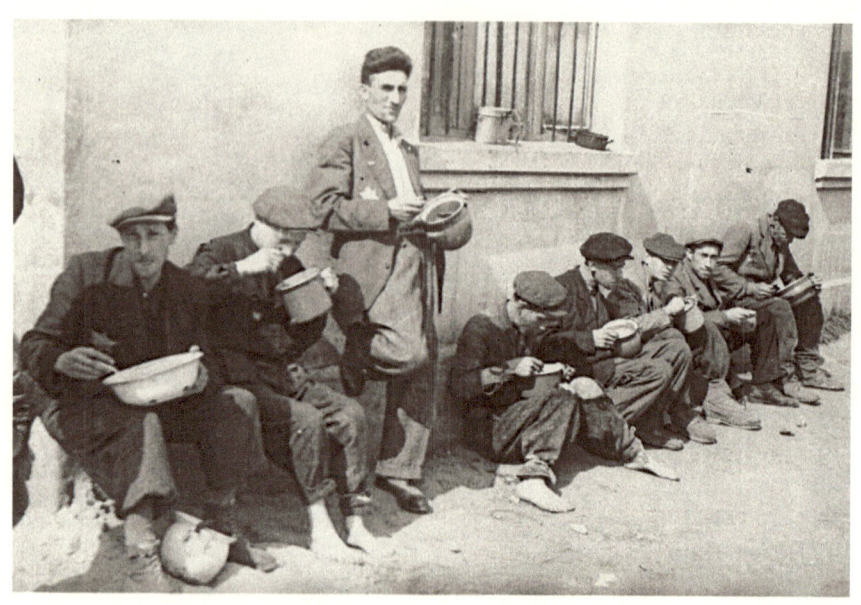

Henryk Ross, *Lodz Ghetto: "Soup for lunch."* 1940–1944.
Print from original 35mm negative. Collection of the
Art Gallery of Ontario, gift from the Archive of Modern
Conflict, 2007. 2007/1967.3.

This little book describes the history and destruction of the Jewish community of a city the Poles call "Łódź" (pronounced "woodzh") and that those who speak other languages generally know and spell as "Lodz" (pronounced "lawch"), a name its one-time German inhabitants spelled as "Lodsch" and its one-time Yiddish-speaking Jewish inhabitants spelled as "לאדזש."

This little book tells a relentlessly depressing story of the systematic destruction of a vibrant community. Like any other community, it included many different people: young and elderly, smart and foolish, beautiful and ugly, successful and unsuccessful, resilient and weak, good and bad, hopeful and hopeless. Together they represented, in the microcosm of their community, the splendid plurality and variety of the human race. Together they embodied the countless possibilities that come with life in general, modern life in particular—with its ideals of liberty bound by law, fraternity amid competition, and equality from difference—and life in a great metropolis above all. Yet this multiplicity of different people became the object of a toxic, phantasmagoric and phantamorgasmic delusion that opposed the idea that the glory of humanity is to be found in its plenitude and plurality, and that defined the members of that community—young and elderly, smart and foolish, beautiful and ugly, and so on—merely as aspects of a single malign disease that ought to be rooted out from the earth. The champions of this radically evil sham set out to destroy this community, working hard to create conditions in which all of those different people were plunged to the lowest bottom, where life could persist only in a primordial equality that knows neither fraternity nor humanity—a life that then could be extinguished without a second thought as to whether all, or even any, deserved such a fate.

This little book tells a lopsided story about the destruction of a community. If it were to do justice to the nature, scale and scope of the catastrophe, it would devote hundreds of thousands of pages to record the hundreds of thousands of unique lives that were thus extinguished, and offer a single paragraph to the evil delusion that caused this tragedy. Knowledge of even one of those lives enriches our lives, while information about that monstrous libel does not. Yet as members of a community in which we are confronted daily with the pleasures and challenges that come with living amid a plurality of people, we do not really need to know all those biographies to know that each human being is created, as the Bible puts it, in the image and likeness of God, and that the murder of any one person equals, as the Jewish sages put it, the destruction of the world. This book assumes that you, the reader, remembers that each and every member of that community is not just a statistic, but remains an essential part of a plurality that encompasses not only the living—young and elderly, smart and foolish, beautiful and ugly, and so on—but also the dead, and the as yet unborn. It assumes, in other words, a basic understanding of the human condition. But it cannot assume knowledge of the concoction that, like a dream that evaporates in the morning, has no reality in the here and now, and does not belong to the life we share. Because it is an absurd figment of the imagination, because it has no roots in reality, it needs more attention than it really deserves. Such is the paradox of writing history.

This little book tells the story of a city where, until the fall of 1939, Poles, Germans and Jews rubbed shoulders—a city of occasional ethnic friction, but little ethnic collision.[1] It was a remarkable city, quite unlike any other in Poland. *"Ich bin in Lodz: Fabriken, Wildwest, Provinz"* ("I'm in Lodz: factories, the Wild West, the sticks"), the German Jewish physician and author Alfred Döblin wrote in October 1924.[2] Factories: rational determination; the Wild West: lawlessness; the sticks: narrow horizons. Many believe that Döblin caught in these three powerful and clashing images the essence of that most exasperating and also intriguing of cities—a city where, until the fall of 1939, Jews such as the poet Julian Tuwim (who wrote in Polish and not in Yiddish) felt at home: *"Niech sobie Ganges, Sorrento, Krym / Pod niebo inni wynoszą, / A ja Łódź wolę! Jej brud i dym / Szczęściem mi są i rozkoszą"* ("Let others debate the merits / Of the Ganges, Sorrento, or the Crimea / Give me Lodz! Her dirt and smoke / Bring happiness and delight to me").[3] Then Nazi Germany attacked Poland, conquered the western part, incorporated Łódź/Lodz/Lodsch/לאדזש into the Greater German Reich, renamed it "Litzmannstadt," imprisoned the Jews in a ghetto sealed from the world—a captive population and a town-size prison Henryk Rozencwajg-Ross (1910–1991) and Mendel Grossman (1913–1945) were to photograph over an almost four-year period. The Germans allowed a quarter of the inmates to die from starvation, turning the ghetto into what those who knew the conditions within its walls contemptuously referred to as the *"Krepierwinkel Europas"* ("croaking hole of Europe"),[4] and killed the rest in Herbert Lange's gas vans stationed at the village of Kulmhof, known by the Poles as Chełmno nad Nerem (1942–1944), and in the Auschwitz-Birkenau crematoria (1944).

"All books are divisible into two classes, the books of the hour, and the books of all time,"[5] John Ruskin once wrote. This little book is unapologetically a book of the hour. It was written to provide context for an exhibition, at the Art Gallery of Ontario (AGO) in Toronto, of the mostly unauthorized photographs Ross made in the Lodz Ghetto—the negatives of which are in the AGO's collection. Employed by the Statistics Department of the ghetto's *Judenrat* (Jewish Council), Ross and his colleague Grossman were charged with taking portraits of ghetto officials, documenting official meetings, producing passport-sized photographs of every ghetto inmate for identity cards, making a visual record of unidentified corpses abandoned in the ghetto streets, tracking physical changes in the ghetto as buildings were pulled down, and chronicling the efficiency of the ghetto workshops. While explicitly forbidden from the end of 1941 onward to make any personal or private photographs, both Ross and Grossman regularly ventured out in the ghetto to record ghetto life as lived, at risk of imprisonment and, during the great deportations, risk of life.[6]

Prints of pictures Grossman took in the ghetto survive, but the 10,000 negatives Grossman, his sister Fajga Frajtag and his friend August Ben-Menachem buried in the ghetto before his deportation to a concentration camp in Germany were destroyed. Grossman did not survive the Holocaust, but Frajtag and Ben-Menachem did. Frajtag recovered the negatives in 1945 and sent them to Ben-Menachem, who had already moved to Palestine to join Kibbutz Nitzanim. During Israel's War of Independence, the Egyptian Army captured and levelled Nitzanim, and all the negatives were lost. Were they destroyed or taken as booty? There are speculations that they survive somewhere in Egypt.[7]

The negatives of the unauthorized photos Ross made did survive. "In July 1944, when I heard and saw that the ghetto was about to be liquidated, that they were going to expel all of us, I hid the negatives in barrels and concealed them in the ground," Ross told the Jerusalem Court sitting in judgment of former Gestapo official Adolf Eichmann in 1961. "Did you succeed in saving some of the negatives and bring them with you to Israel?" prosecutor Gideon Hausner asked Ross. "Yes," Ross replied. "Some were destroyed owing to water seeping in, but the greater part was saved."[8]

Ross's negatives have proved an enormous treasure. But not all of the photos were welcome. The images of people who were at the bottom end of the ghetto hierarchy because they were "useless mouths" as well as the images of people who provided the middle classes because they had the skills and strength to put in twelve-hour days in exchange for 800 calories were useful to the Jerusalem court and easily integrated into the Jewish collective memory of the Holocaust. But what to do with the images of the few who belonged to the ghetto elite, the members and families of the ghetto administration and the *Ordnungsdienst* (Order Service), the Jewish ghetto police? What to do with the visual evidence of these privileged Jews spending merry moments with colleagues, friends and family? This part of the Ross collection remained a no-go area until 2004, when British documentary photographer Martin Parr, photographer and curator Timothy Prus and historian Thomas Weber published a small selection of the more controversial images.[9]

This little book provides a context in which to understand these photographs, which show that, within a situation designed to create complete equality in misery, some form of plurality remained—a plurality that was achieved at a price that might have included some form of collaboration, if not directly with the German rulers, then certainly with the German-imposed *Judenrat*, headed by the notorious Mordechai Chaim Rumkowski. These images show a persistence of multiplicity in the second-largest ghetto created during the Nazi Holocaust of the Jews (1939–1945). One of the questions this book seeks to answer is how some measure of plurality managed to persist amid the grinding conditions imposed by the Germans.

Where to begin? Perhaps a direction can be found by considering the subject of Ross's photos: life in the Lodz Ghetto. What is a ghetto, or better, what was the ghetto in Nazi-ruled Europe? "The authorities of the Third Reich never actually defined the term ghetto," historians Guy Miron and Shlomit Shulhani observe in the introduction to *The Yad Vashem Encyclopedia of the Ghettos During the Holocaust* (2009). "We have defined as a ghetto any part of a pre-existing settlement occupied by Nazi Germany where Jews were forcibly confined for at least a few weeks."[10] The adjective "pre-existing" is key: during the Holocaust, Germans and their allies also confined Jews to camps. Each of the many types of camps used to imprison Jews was without local precedent, unlike the German-imposed ghettos, which had clear relations to pre-war Jewish neighbourhoods. The Nazi official who took the initiative to establish the Lodz Ghetto, Friedrich Uebelhoer, stressed the importance of precedent in a description of the creation of that ghetto: "We have taken the most effective but also the most radical action by expelling the Jews in Litzmannstadt to the district—namely the ghetto—from which they had poured over the city in earlier times," he wrote in 1941.[11]

In other words: the Lodz Ghetto was not a creation *ex nihilo*. It arose in a local context that included a historical ghetto from which the Jews had emerged "in earlier times" and to which they were returned under German rule. This suggests that any understanding of the history of the Lodz Ghetto must reach back to the time of that original settlement of Jews in Lodz, which coincides with the beginning of the industrial development of the city as a centre of textile production.

In addition, the expulsion of the Jews to their place of origin happened in a larger ideological context. The German propaganda pictures that illustrated Uebelhoer's text were captioned by a single sentence that concisely summarized the Nazi *Weltanschauung* (world view) concerning the Jews, and hence the ideological foundation of the Holocaust: "The vital nerve of International Jewry has been hit in Litzmannstadt."[12] The idea that Jews in Lodz had been brought back to a point of origin and the idea that the internment of the Jews in that city would radically weaken "International Jewry"—whatever that might be—seemed vitally important to Uebelhoer. It appears we may gain some understanding of the purpose of the ghetto not only by considering the pre-1939 history of Lodz in some detail, with a special focus on where Jews lived and the relative size of the Jewish community in relation to other communities, but also by gaining an understanding of the Nazi *Weltanschauung* in which "International Jewry" could be choked by imprisoning the Lodz Jews.

This little book does not tell a happy tale. But it is an important one, and perhaps even an urgent one, as it is told in a time in which the old phantasmagoria that created the Nazi Holocaust of the Jews seems to have gained new life—and not only in the Middle East, but also in Europe and, to a lesser extent, North America. This is indeed, and sadly, a book of the hour.

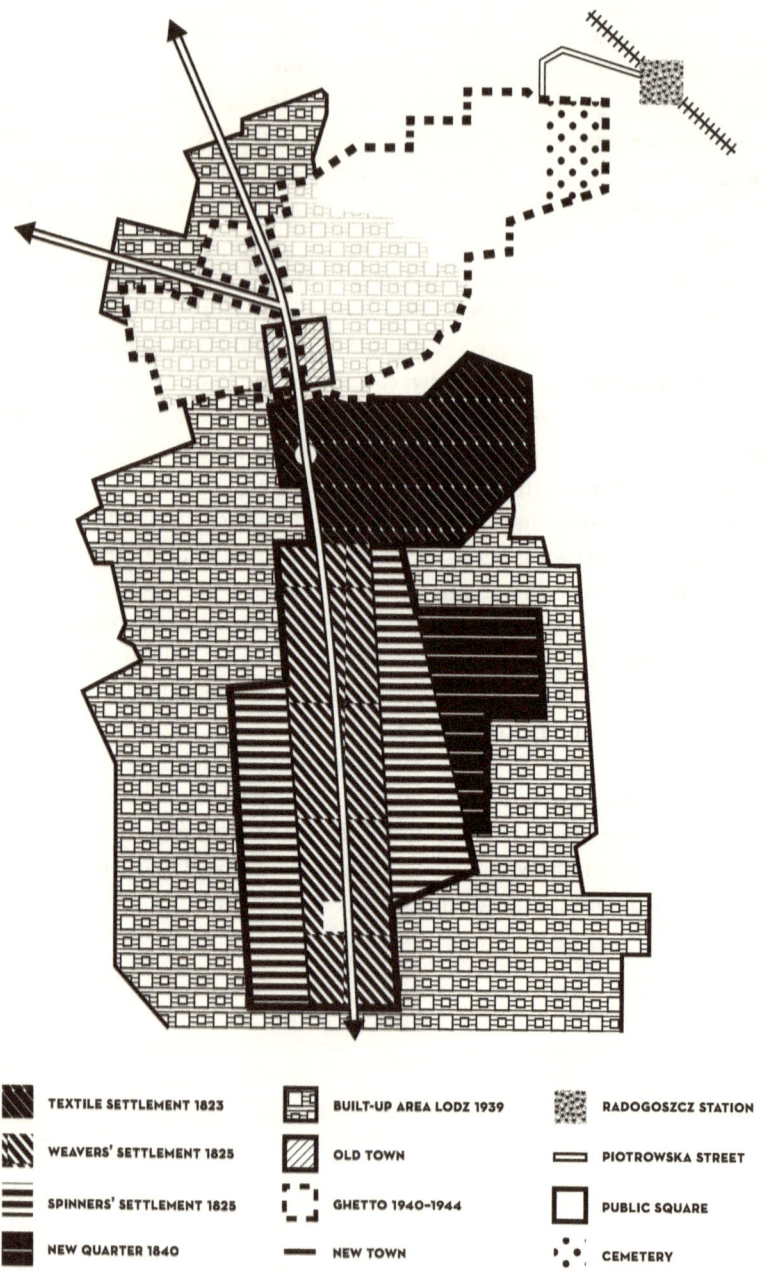

Map of the development of Lodz, by Department of Unusual Certainties.

CHAPTER ONE

Promised Land

Mentioned for the first time in the early fourteenth century and granted in the fifteenth century a charter as a town, Lodz remained a somewhat overgrown village until the early nineteenth century, when the Congress of Vienna, which rearranged Europe in the wake of Napoleon's defeats in Leipzig and Waterloo, allocated the town to the Kingdom of Poland, which was also informally known as "Congress Poland." As the crown of this kingdom was given to Czar Alexander, Emperor and Autocrat of All the Russias, Congress Poland became first an autonomous part of the Russian Empire, and then, as the nineteenth century progressed, an increasingly less autonomous *General-Gubernatorstvo* (General Governorate). (During the German and Austrian occupation of 1915–1918, and the German occupation of 1939–1945, this originally Russian designation was to survive in the designation "Generalgouvernement" for those Polish territories that were occupied but not annexed.)

Incorporation into the Russian Empire brought economic opportunity: German entrepreneurs rightly reasoned that they could access the huge Russian market, protected by custom tariffs, by establishing wool and linen mills in Lodz, which was located close to the Prussian and Austrian borders and, due to many freshwater springs, had an ample supply of clean water—a key requirement for textile production. From 1823 onward, German weavers from Westphalia, Silesia and Bohemia settled in a series of colonies aligned along the main road that connected Lodz to the provincial capital, Piotrków Trybunalski, known as "Petrikau" by the German settlers. These settlements became collectively known as "Neustadt" or "Nowe Miasta" ("New Town"), and the original town of Lodz became known as the "Altstadt" or "Stare Miasta" ("Old Town"). The three-mile-long spine that adjoined the settlement of the New Town was named "Petrikauer Straße" or "Ulica Piotrkowska" (commonly referred to in English as either "Petrikov Street" or "Piotrkowska Street").[1]

In 1848, some of the restrictions on Jewish residency in the towns of Russian Poland were abolished. Now Jewish craftsmen from Austrian-ruled Galicia to the south began to arrive in Lodz to join the small Jewish congregation that had been in existence since the beginning of the century.[2] Unless they had substantial capital and were willing to assimilate, these Jewish immigrants were not allowed to settle in the New Town, which they knew as "נײ טאָטש" (pronounced "nay-shtot"). Thus they moved into the Old Town, known as "טלאָ טאָטש" ("alt-shtot"), or the adjacent village of Bałuty, which they knew as "טולאָב" ("Balut"). By 1859, the Jewish community was both large and wealthy enough to begin construction of a substantial synagogue in the Moorish style. Only in 1862 did the authorities open up the New Town. Jews moved in from the Old Town, as did Polish peasants from nearby rural areas who until then had been restricted in their movements. The majority of the Jews moving into the New Town were craftsmen, shopkeepers and merchants, while the majority of the Poles became factory workers.[3]

Between 1814 and 1914, the average annual growth rate was an astonishing 7 per cent, transforming Lodz from a village-size town with 767 inhabitants into a metropolis of half a million inhabitants. Key events in the growth of the city were the construction of the first steam engine–powered weaving plant (1835), the elimination of the last remaining custom boundary between Congress Poland and the rest of the Russian Empire (1850), and the Crimean War, which brought an end to cotton imports from Great Britain and led to the construction of Lodz's first cotton-spinning mill (1854). From that date onward, Lodz became a place of ferocious opportunity and competition. Fuelled by ambition and greed, the city offered to some the rapture of fortunes made, and to more the shame of fortunes lost. It seemed almost American in its promise to transform rags into riches amid a melting pot of three ethnicities, which in the rest of the Polish lands remained locked in either open conflict or, at least, distrust and antipathy.

Wladislaw Stanislaw Reymont described this Lodz in his *Ziemia Obiecana* (1898), translated as *The Promised Land*.[4] Its three young protagonists are the German Max Baum, the Jew Moritz Welt and the Polish aristocrat Karol Borowiecki. "I have no money; neither have you. Nor has he," Max tells Moritz and Karol at the beginning of the story. "So," he concludes, "we have just enough, just exactly enough to start quite a big factory."[5] This was the "can-do" attitude that characterized the *Lodzermensch* (Lodzian), an optimistic, opportunistic and ruthless risk-taker who was quite willing to ignore traditional boundaries if it helped him compete in a global world. Reality transcended fiction: the life and times of a Jewish entrepreneur like Izrael Kalmanowicz Poznański became the stuff of legend. And unlike the fictional Baum, Welt and Borowiecki, Poznański did engage in charitable activities, building and maintaining synagogues, schools, hospitals and orphanages.

Charities provided a necessary valve in the pressure cooker that was Lodz. *Lodzermenschen* were ruthless in their dealings with the workers in their factories, who, in turn, became radicalized to form the avant-garde in the workers' movement in the Russian Empire, engaging in lengthy strikes that the entrepreneurs violently quelled with the help of the ever-ready Cossacks. Seeing Lodz capitalism at work turned Rosa Luxemburg into a Marxist. "So far, Lodz is a city that is reminiscent of the settlements that were quickly built next to the gold mines in Australia and America," she observed. Inhabited by many people of different cultural and ethnic backgrounds, it was a community without a foundation. In the other great cities created by the Industrial Revolution, the older elites, the bourgeoisie and the new capitalist entrepreneurs shared language, history and culture. "The Lodz manufacturers, however, are a composite mixture with a variety of backgrounds, cultures and nationalities, and although they determine to some extent the political and social life in our country, they have absolutely no contact with Polish culture, take no part in so-called polite society, and are only connected to it by the desire for profit and robbery," Luxemburg wrote.[6] She did not take the philanthropy of *Lodzermenschen* seriously, because, as a Marxist, she believed not in social service but in social change.

The skyline of Lodz manifested the city's lack of social order and cohesion: huge factories with countless chimneys adjoined the vulgar estates of the industrialists, which in turn adjoined the meanest of tenements; first-class hotels rubbed shoulders with murky barracks; fancy restaurants jostled with dilapidated hovels; proud churches pushed against melancholy warehouses; and tottering cottages leaned against splendid synagogues. In short: opulence mixed effortlessly with destitution, and vice versa. And only in Lodz did a tenement building become a lavish palace: with the ruthless efficiency for which he was known, Poznański ordered architects Juliusz Jung and Dawid Rosenthal to use the workers' housing, which stood on a lot he had bought, as the core of the neo-Baroque Poznański Palace, one of the largest private residences built in the nineteenth century. And yet Poznański instructed architect Hilary Majewski to build what was to be the most monumental cotton mill in Congress Poland from scratch. Today, the sixty-acre Poznański Factory is known as the "Manufaktura," and encompasses a vibrant shopping and cultural district.

A puzzling city—promised land? It certainly was for a man like Poznański. But for all too many, the city proved a trap. Polish writer Zygmunt Bartkiewicz coined a different name when he wrote his own novel about Lodz: *Złe miasto* (1907), translated as *Evil City*. And the workers who slaved in the factories had another moniker for Lodz: "*Przedsionek do Piekła*," or "Antechamber to Hell."[7]

The rise of Lodz was due to the immigration of Germans, and their descendants remembered that their ancestors had brought the first looms to the town, initiated the mechanization of textile production, and built the mills that had established the city's reputation as the Manchester of Eastern Europe. They did not forget that, in 1840, Germans constituted almost four-fifths of the town's population. By the end of the century, the German, Polish and Jewish populations of the city were of roughly equal size, while by 1914 Poles made up half of the population, Jews a third and Germans a sixth. The German community was, per capita, perhaps wealthier, but the Jewish community had the largest footprint in the local economy: in 1914 Jewish entrepreneurs controlled 40 per cent of the textile production, and most of the city's commerce and finance. After seventy-five years of relative decline, the Germans in Lodz resented the Jewish community—especially because this upstart population had come to dominate the cultural life of the city. Germans, of course, had cultivated since the early nineteenth century a self-image of being a people of *Dichter und Denker* (poets and philosophers), but in Lodz it was the Jews who prevailed in the arts and publishing and set the tone in theatres, galleries and concert halls. Virtuoso pianist Artur Rubinstein was born in Lodz. His father owned a textile mill, and the family lived on Piotrkowska Street.

While a small part of the Jewish community was wealthy and prominent in the social and cultural life of the city, the great majority was poor. Many of the Jews who had arrived in the city came from the non-Polish parts of Russia, where they had suffered from 1882 onward government-initiated pogroms. These had triggered a flight westward, and while most of the Jewish refugees had ended up in North America, significant numbers had settled in metropolitan European cities such as London and Berlin. Lodz provided an uncertain haven within the Russian Empire as a new and virulent strain of anti-Semitism, based on a fiction peddled by the Russian secret police, began to influence the views of non-Jews trying to understand the puzzling changes that came with modernization.

Reinterpreting French conspiracy theories that postulated that key historical events in general—and the great convulsions of the French Revolution in particular—had been prepared and controlled by a tight-knit, self-perpetuating group of conspirators such as the so-called Illuminati or the Freemasons, Russian secret policemen, worried about the rise of revolutionary movements that aimed to overthrow the Czar, developed a narrative that Jews were the authors of some secret, nefarious and global scheme to undermine the natural order of things. This story, entitled *The Protocols of the Elders of Zion*, began to appear in bookshops throughout the Russian Empire in 1903. It was a bestseller by 1914.[8]

In August 1914, a war broke out that pitted, among others, Russia against Germany. As a matter of course, the Russian authorities arrested citizens of the German Reich and deported them to the east. Some 200,000 Germans of Russian citizenship living in Volhynia were also arrested on the grounds that they might be spies, and their possessions were plundered. Their fate destroyed the trust of those of German descent living in Russia that the Russian government had their best interests at heart, and it encouraged pan-German sentiments in many of those who before 1914 had been loyal and even proud subjects of the Czar. The Lodzer Germans were spared deportation: by the time the Russians decided to remove all Germans from the actual and expected zones of battle, Lodz was already occupied in the wake of a battle in which a German army, commanded by General Karl Litzmann, defeated strong Russian forces aiming to capture Berlin. The Battle of Lodz led to the German occupation of the city, which was to last until November 1918.

The occupation meant a catastrophe for the economy. Separated from their market, the textile barons closed most of their production lines, and all the inhabitants of Lodz—Poles, Germans and Jews—went through difficult times. Many nationalistically inclined Poles believed that a German victory would offer political opportunities for the revival of a Polish national state, and they tended to support a policy of collaboration with the German Army of Occupation. The German inhabitants of Lodz became increasingly patriotic about their German ancestry and identity. Sermons given by German army chaplains aroused nationalistic sentiments, and an early sign of the new jingoism was the name change of the German-language *Lodzer Zeitung* (*Lodz Daily*) to *Deutsche Lodzer Zeitung* (*German Lodz Daily*). A newly established newspaper received the name *Deutsche Post* (*German Post*). In addition to providing news, this publication also aimed to awaken the German residents of the city to their heritage: "In response to German book and pamphlet writers, who described Lodz as a purely Polish city, it was necessary to provide proof of the debt owed by both the Lodz industrial area and the heart of Poland, Warsaw, to German diligence and efficiency.... It was necessary to enlighten those who had been badly taught, and fill our Lodz Germans with a new pride for the achievements of their fathers, and to also provide them with encouragement."[9] The German inhabitants of Lodz began to see themselves as Germans, first and foremost.

They organized themselves in the *Deutscher Verein für Lodz und Umgegend* (German Association for Lodz and Surroundings), which aimed not only to awaken within the Germans living in Lodz pride in the German character of the city, but also to educate those living in the German Reich about the pioneering work done by Germans in Lodz. Many other organizations that carried the adjective "German" in their name followed.

At this time, the German inhabitants of Lodz identified the Russian government as their enemy and the Polish majority population as their main rival. They did not care that much about the Jewish population of the city. The German Army of Occupation also left the Lodz Jews alone. But while the German soldiers patrolling along Piotrkowska did not care much about the Jews they encountered, German civilians in Berlin considered the tens of thousands of destitute, hungry, filthy and ill Jewish refugees arriving from the German-occupied areas of Polish Russia with anxiety and fear: these *Ostjuden* (eastern Jews) seemed an utterly alien people who could never be integrated. Their presence charged existing anti-Semitic prejudices with a particular urgency, and defining them as carriers of typhus, the German government began to deport those arriving at the border, those who had been able to reach German cities, and those who had been arrested for even the most minor violation of the law to German-occupied Poland. Immediately after the end of the war, the German authorities added another tool to their kit: in the towns of Cottbus-Sielow and Stargard in Pommern (today Stargard Szczeciński), they created in former prisoner-of-war camps *Konzentrationslager für Ausländer* (concentration camps for foreigners) to accommodate the stateless *Ostjuden* before expelling them to the now-sovereign Polish state. These were the first concentration camps on German soil. The authorities were content: the new *Ostjudenfrage* (Question of the eastern Jews) had received its proper answer: deportation and internment in concentration camps.[10]

The Germans in general and the German government in particular were not alone in their concern about the *Ostjudenfrage*. German Jews considered their destitute cousins from Poland with both pity and anxiety. Since the early nineteenth century, German Jews had attempted to find a place in an increasingly nationalistic Germany through acculturation: by accepting middle-class notions of improvement through education and cultural and social refinement, they hoped to be accepted by Christian society as genuine Germans, be it of the *Mosaïsche* (Mosaic) religion. This process of acculturation and, at times, even assimilation demanded a rejection of many traditional aspects of Jewish life, represented by the Jews from Poland. The German Jewish philosopher Moses

Mendelsohn contemptuously defined Yiddish as a "jargon" and "a language of stammers, corrupt and deformed, repulsive to those who are able to speak in a correct and elegant manner"[11]—a judgment that became dominant in nineteenth-century German Jewish society. But if the Jews from Poland were the focus of more than mere curiosity, it was only as objects of paternalistic schemes of improvement. And there seemed to be much to improve: in 1816, the German Jew David Friedländer argued in his *Über die Verbesserung der Israeliten im Königreich Pohlen* (*On the Improvement of the Israelites in the Kingdom of Poland*) that "the Polish Jews are generally considered to be the most cloddish and unrefined class of human beings who stand, in terms of culture and morality, on the lowest level, next to savages"[12]—a condition which, incidentally, Friedländer considered to be the result not of some innate character flaw, but of the abject social isolation in which the Polish Jews were kept.

Among the majority of German Jews, dismissive attitudes toward *Ostjuden* had hardened in the late nineteenth century, when their cousins from the east began to arrive in Berlin and other German cities. The miserable plight of the Jewish refugees from Poland who streamed into Berlin during the Great War did not change their views. In 1922, the German Jewish author Jakob Wasserman articulated the general view of acculturated German Jews toward the *Ostjuden*: "Whenever I encountered a Polish or Galician Jew, talked to him, and made an effort to grasp his inner being, to understand his way of life and thinking, I might become compassionate, or curious, or even feel sadness, yet I never felt a sense of brotherhood, and not even of kinship. In the way he expressed himself, and even in the way he was breathing, he was entirely strange, and when there was no individual human sympathy, he was even repulsive."[13] To be fair: German Jewish philosophers like Hermann Cohen, Franz Rosenzweig and Martin Buber were fascinated by the Polish Jews because they thought this community might have preserved an authentic ethnic, social or religious core, and they believed that the future of Judaism and the Jewish people was to be found in a synthesis between the *Ostjüdische* roots in folklore and tradition and the German Jewish immersion in European culture. "A great deal of genuine Judaism is still alive within him," Cohen wrote in a celebrated article on the Polish Jew.

> On account of this, we must not despair that he will himself bring us salvation if he continues in even larger numbers than before to return to our lands, from which many of his number once migrated [in the fourteenth century]. With an almost superhuman endurance, which he has tried and

tested, he will add a new impetus to our ideal ethics, our willingness to make sacrifices for spiritual tasks. And his acute intelligence and intuitive capacity make him the right person to sharpen us, temper us, and spur us on to intellectual trials of skill. For, among us, the effects of Talmudic dialectics are unfortunately lapsing. But in Eastern Europe, they are as fresh as ever.[14]

Many German Jewish youngsters rebelled against their over-assimilated parents not only by becoming Zionists but also by proclaiming their own romanticized view of the *Ostjuden*'s ways as an ideal of the good Jewish life. And some German Jews tried to act in accordance with the core teaching of Judaism—one that was first articulated in the book of Exodus: "וְגֵר לֹא תוֹנֶה וְלֹא תִלְחָצֶנּוּ כִּי גֵרִים הֱיִיתֶם בְּאֶרֶץ מִצְרָיִם" ("You must not mistreat or oppress foreigners in any way. Remember, you yourselves were once foreigners in the land of Egypt").[15] It was a teaching that had been brought into rigorous philosophical focus by the very same Hermann Cohen who believed that Polish Jewry could bring new vitality to German Jewish intellectual culture. The Torah taught, Cohen argued, that the alien was to be protected, not because of family bonds, clan membership or a common religion, but because he was a fellow human being, created by God in his image and likeness. This was expressed in the biblical concept that, in the eyes of the law, the stranger was equal to the native-born member of the Israelite community. "It is a massive advance that signals the birth of the concept of humanity," Cohen concluded.[16] These cousins from the east were, of course, not fully strangers. After all, they were members of the same ethnic group and shared the same religion. But it appears that Sigmund Freud's concept of *der Narzißmus der kleinen Differenzen* (the narcissism of small differences) applied to the attitude of the great majority of German Jews: they looked at the *Ostjuden* with a measure of contempt and acted toward them at best in a spirit of charity.

And then there was fear—fear that the manifest poverty of the *Ostjuden* would change the attitudes of the Germans toward all Jews. This concern appeared justified in the light of subsequent developments. "It is no exaggeration to say that the injection from the east had strengthened the Jewish organism, but also completely ruined its relation to the host nation," Oskar Singer observed in 1942—a few months after his deportation from Prague to Lodz. He added, "While initially western Jewry had generously offered help and hospitality to the brother from the East—the countless Jewish aid committees in all the cities are still in our memories—inevitably a reaction arose that expressed itself in a violent dislike of the *Ostjude*—a dislike often increased to open hostility. Even the binding, reconciling Zionist idea failed to bridge the gulf that quickly opened. The idea of Jewish unity has suffered a severe shock from which it has not yet recovered." For Singer there was no doubt: the rise of German anti-Semitism in the 1920s had been a direct result of the increased presence of the *Ostjuden* in German cities, and his reflections manifest the bitterness with which many German Jews deported to the Lodz Ghetto considered the *Ostjuden*, and not Nazi madness, the cause of their demise. Singer also noted that the *Ostjude* had not forgotten the patronizing attitude of his cousins from the west; he remembered how he had felt despised, something that made no sense because the *Ostjude* knew that he, and not the assimilated Jew in the west, constituted the future of the Jewish nation. "He responded with pride," Singer wrote, to which he added a second emotion: "hate." And, Singer concluded: "He waited for his hour."[17]

In the fall of 1918, the Germans faced defeat in the west, and in the east, Polish nationalists proclaimed a sovereign Polish state. The core was Congress Poland, which was enlarged through agreement or conquest by other territories formerly part of the Russian, Austro-Hungarian and German empires. Of particular importance for the future of Lodz was the incorporation into Poland of the Posen province, which had belonged first to Prussia and since 1793 to the German Reich. While the Posen (or, as it was known in Polish, "Poznań") region had an ethnic Polish majority in the rural areas, the city of Posen was German to the core, and both its population and the German government in Berlin resented the transfer and vowed to revise it at some future date. Lodz became the second-largest city in this new state. This incorporation certainly bolstered the confidence of the Polish population of the city: while they had constituted Lodz's largest ethnic group since the late nineteenth century, the Poles had never had the prestige or wealth of either the Germans or the Jews.

Yet pre-war prosperity did not return. The textile industry remained in dire straits: created to serve the huge pre-war Russian market, its capacity was too large for the relatively small Polish market. In addition, the industrialists lacked the capital needed to retool their operations: before 1914 they had deposited their capital and securities in Russian banks, and the Bolshevik government had seized all financial assets. Economically, Lodz slid into a depression. *"Reymont nazwał Łódź 'ziemią obiecaną.' Bartkiewicz—'złem miastem'"* ("Reymont called Lodz 'promised land,' Bartkiewicz—'evil town'"), Tuwim lamented in 1934. "Today, all of this means nothing. The city experiences a tragedy. A colossus and at the same time a pauper, a giant in a state of vegetation, whose immense size has lost both meaning and justification. A city without tradition, without local legends, without a mythology; a city that is not connected with the history and the culture of the nation."[18] The *Lodzermensch*, who had been a miracle man when the city was growing, became in the era of economic depression an object of scorn. A Polish encyclopedia published in the 1930s defined him as "a type of Lodz businessman, who gained profits under German-Jewish influence, and has no national identity and focuses only on his money-making."[19]

Döblin agreed. When he visited Lodz, he encountered *Lodzermenschen* who still believed in the big gamble that would make all things right, and he did not like them: "Two men converse across from me at the table. 'In Lodz, only the big numbers catch on, anything else is completely worthless in Lodz.' What do they mean? Coats, actions, people? They whisper very mysteriously; now they turn their backs on me. I don't understand: How come only big numbers catch on in Lodz? How come? Dark things are afoot in Lodz." Döblin was more attuned to the unique cosmopolitan and multicultural charms that could be observed while walking the length of the main drag, from south to north. "Elderly gentlemen glance at women coming toward them," he wrote. "How incredibly painted they are. Beauty spots on their chins or in the corners of their mouths. Their black coats are pulled tight around their waists and rears, and their buttonholes sport glaring red roses, broad, wild, luxurious floral creatures that die, croak on this black cloth, spreading arms and legs in their final agony."[20]

As he approached the Old Town, Döblin noticed that the streetscape changed. Instead of gorgeously dressed women, Jewish men in more traditional garb began to dominate the streetscape. "The further north I go, the more Jews there are: in high fur caps and black fur coats, black skullcaps, with long, thick beards, their hands in their pockets, their feet in top boots; furrowed brows. As in Warsaw, scores of them emerge from deep courtyards." He crossed the New Town Ring, which he judged to be shabby, and then arrived in the Old Town, which had been allocated to the Jews when the New Town was laid out, and which in 1924 constituted an informal "ghetto" where the poorest Jews lived. "The old city, narrow streets, crumbling small houses. I step into a dreadful house, cross the courtyard, pass through a door, find myself in a different street. It's teeming with kids; the ground sinks in waves. Lots of slaughterhouses for geese. A small synagogue is open." Finally, he reached the former village of Bałuty, which had absorbed from the 1850s onward the overflow of poor Jews from the Old Town, and which had been annexed to the city in 1915. "In a wretched lane, I'm told, there are many prostitutes, pimps, and thieves; the lane is badly paved; there are miserable houses."[21]

Both the economic decline and a general unwillingness to adapt to life as a minority in a Polish national state encouraged many Germans to sell their businesses and homes and emigrate to the German Reich. By the end of the 1920s, the relative size of the Polish, Jewish and German populations in the city was eight to four to one. As their community was in a slow state of collapse, the remaining Germans increasingly began to listen to anyone who offered an explanation. One prevailed. In 1924, as he walked along Piotrkowska, Döblin encountered a bookshop. "The bookshop has two windows," he wrote. "I ignore the Polish one with its hieroglyphs. Then, two paces to the left: *Die Sünde wider das Blut—The Sin Against the Blood*. I can read this. I don't have to translate it. Ah, I'm home again, a thousand greetings.... *Die Sünde wider das Blut*; a whole row. *Lauter deutsche Worte, kerndeutsche Worte*—Nothing but German words, German to the core!" There were also copies of another book in the window, a new gospel. "I see: the swastika on the cover, and the name of a German nationalistic agitator above it. His Gospels! His! Yes, that's good, now I'm in the picture, now there's order in the shop window."[22]

The city of Lodz was hit heavily by the Great Depression, which began in late 1929. In Lodz production hit bottom in 1934, when total employment in the textile industry was a mere 60,000. A recovery followed, but this was led not by the large industries but by many very small enterprises created with much *chutzpah* and minimal capital investment in the empty hulks of massive factories that had gone bankrupt—it was messy, but it got people to work again. Yet because many of the new entrepreneurs were Jews, and because Germans had owned some of the large factories in which they set up shop, the economic revival was seen by the German community as a prime example of Jews profiting from German decline.[23]

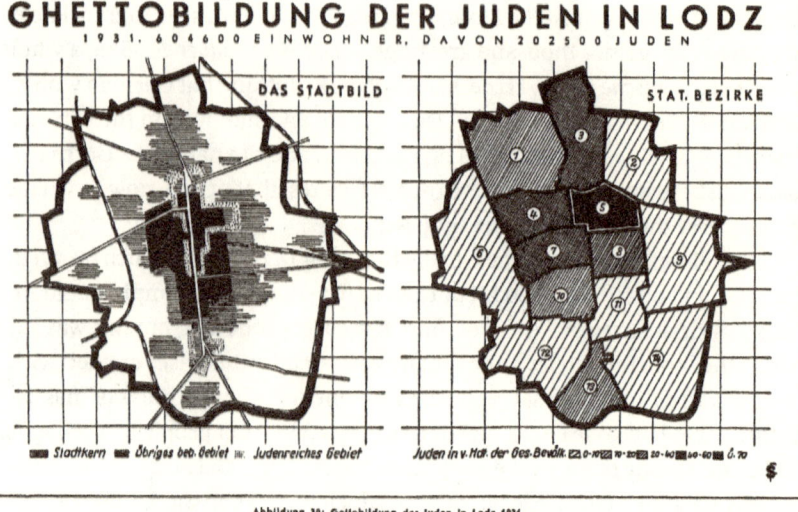

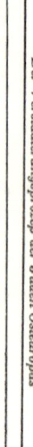

Abbildung 30: Gettobildung der Juden in Lodz 1931

Maps of the Jewish expansion in Lodz, by Peter-Heinz Seraphim.
Collection of the author.

CHAPTER TWO
A Jewish Question

A new, vicious and virulent form of racial anti-Semitism had grown in Germany in the wake of the Great War, and it inspired many Lodz Germans in the 1920s, '30s and '40s. This strain of prejudice was the direct offspring of the confrontation with the destitute *Ostjuden* that had begun to dominate the streets in certain Berlin neighbourhoods after 1914, the sudden military and political collapse of November 1918, and the publication of a German translation of *The Protocols of the Elders of Zion*, which provided an explanation for that collapse.

Alfred Rosenberg, a German born and raised in Russia who moved to Germany after the triumph of Bolshevism, and who was to play a decisive role in shaping Nazi ideology, made *The Protocols* into a primer of the Nazi understanding of the so-called *Judenfrage* (Jewish Question). "*Der Jude*" ("The Jew"), Rosenberg declared, polluted and undermined the human spirit and consequently threatened the very existence of humankind. *Der Jude* could not be modified or integrated: it had to be erased from the earth for the sake of human survival. "Never before have we really understood this," he wrote. "For the first time in history instinct and insight unite in a clear understanding. As a result the Jew, standing on the highest pinnacle of power that he so greedily ascended, faces the abyss. The last fall. After that fall there will be no place anymore for the Jew in Europe."[1]

A political agitator of Austrian birth living in Germany, Adolf Hitler, bought into the fantasy peddled by Rosenberg: the idea that *der Jude*, or the *internationales Judentum* (International Jewry), or the *Weltjudentum* (World-Jewry) sought to rule the world became the bedrock of his *Weltanschauung*. Yet Hitler, and those who shared his *Weltanschauung*, faced a practical problem: it is difficult to maintain one's devotion to fight an enemy when he remains invisible. It was crucial to make *der Jude* comprehensible and visible. Historian Thomas Weber has convincingly argued that Hitler was probably not a racial anti-Semite before 1919.[2] But once Rosenberg and other mentors convinced Hitler of the existence of a global Jewish conspiracy, he projected back into his earlier history a fictional equivalent to St. Paul's Road to Damascus conversion: an experience of enlightenment during his early days in Vienna. In his autobiographical *Mein Kampf*, written in 1924, he asserts that, before his arrival in Vienna, he had not perceived Jews as Jews, but that in Vienna he had learned to see. "Once, as I was strolling through the Inner City, I suddenly encountered an apparition in a black caftan and black hair locks. Is this a Jew? Was my first thought.... I observed the man furtively and cautiously, but the longer I stared at his foreign face, scrutinizing feature for feature, the more my first question assumed a new form: Is this a German?" It was, supposedly, a revelation: now Hitler began to recognize Jews, and to expand on the paranoid narrative presented in *The Protocols*. "Was there any form of filth or profligacy, particularly in cultural life, without at least one Jew involved in it?" He concluded: "If you cut even cautiously into such an abscess, you found, like a maggot in a rotting body, often dazzled by the sudden light—a kike."[3]

Metaphor proved to be an important tool to make *der Jude* visible. Hitler liked to compare him to a maggot, or a fungus, or tubercle bacillus, clearly suggesting that *der Jude* was both a parasite and the cause of a lethal disease that threatened the life of humankind in general and the German *Volksgemeinschaft* (folk community) in particular. It was an idea that resonated because of the experience of the Great War, in which the authorities had identified the *Ostjuden* as carriers of typhus and other epidemic diseases. And one could make *der Jude* visible by forcefully reversing Jewish history since the French Revolution, by undoing both the assimilation and the integration of Jews into non-Jewish society and by countering the progressive fragmentation of Jewish society. And this was what Hitler was committed to do when, in January 1933, he acquired control over the German Reich. Within two months, Nazis began "spontaneously" marking Jewish businesses with crudely painted Stars of David, burning books that embodied a supposedly Jewish spirit of experiment and progressive ideology, and identifying individuals as Jews by expelling them from civic society and the economy and forcing them first into metaphorical ghettos embodied by compulsory Jewish associations and compulsory Jewish residences, and ultimately into compulsory Jewish communities.[4]

In the German Reich the Nazis pushed Poland's German Jews back into symbolic ghettos with the aim of making them leave the country—a difficult project, as few countries welcomed immigrants during the Great Depression of the 1930s. Following their example, the Germans in Lodz also began to define the Jews as dangerous and inassimilable "others." A German geography teacher in Lodz, Eugen Oskar Kossmann, submitted in 1932 to the Jagiellonian University in Kraków his doctoral dissertation on the spatial history of Lodz.

He described the Old Town and the onetime village of Bałuty as bizarre and threatening worlds:

> You can commence—especially in the area of the former ghetto—long walks through the dark, angled spaces, which make you feel as if you're hiking in underground caves in an exotic oriental world. In fact, they call these private business establishments indeed bazaars, in which niches and wall sections are rented by the yard to each shopkeeper.... Business goes on in the most lively manner, producing distorted faces and loud screams. The dealers stop passers-by on the street, and strong-arm their clients into their shops, or better "vaults," using more or less violence to convince the recalcitrant. During the negotiations the customer often leaves the shop "decisively," and then the seller follows him through the streets, and theatrically demands his return. Multiply this form of negotiation many thousandfolds, and you get a picture of business practices that prevail in the old town.[5]

The Old Town was picturesque, and non-Jews could choose not to enter it. More problematic was the fact that the influence of the Jews did not limit itself to the Old Town: from there it radiated throughout the city. Kossmann described the Jewish advance from the Old Town into the New Town as a concerted campaign of conquest: "In this context it is interesting to observe how the Jews, as they increasingly moved to the south, stripped themselves of their old ghetto appearance, and began to assimilate themselves externally."[6] In other words: in the New Town, Jews had ceased to be recognizable as Jews, but inwardly they had not changed. This was, of course, the message of the anti-Semitic books displayed in the bookshop on Piotrkowska Street: whatever was happening in Lodz was but a single battle in a global and eternal war.

There was little Jews could do in response. Having been confronted for centuries with accusations based on libellous fictions, they had learned that any attempt to disprove these charges was a hopeless task. They prayed to God to protect them, shrugged their shoulders and hoped the menace would go away, or tried to make themselves feel better by mocking it. "*Już w podziemiach synagog wszystko złoto leży. / Amunicje przenoszą czarni przemytnicy. /Naradzają się szeptem berlińscy bankierzy, /Dzwoni tajny telefon z warszawskiej bożnicy*" ("Already a large hoard of gold rests in the synagogue cellars. / Black smugglers have delivered ammunition. / Berlin bankers deliberate in whispers / Secret telephone calls from the Warsaw temple"): these are the first lines of "The Anonymous Power," a brilliant and satirical poem in which Tuwim mocks the fantasies that began to take hold of the imagination of his German neighbours. *"W Londynie, w wielkiej loży, już postanowiono… / Siedem pieczęci kładą masoni pod dekret. / Nad skrwawionym Talmudem żółte świece płoną, / W płachtę zwinęli szczątki i przysięgli secret"* ("In London, in the great lodge, all has been decided / The freemasons attach seven seals to the decree. / Yellow candles drip on a blood-spattered Talmud, / Everything is enfolded in canvas as the secret is sworn").[7]

Yet the threat did not pass: too many Germans took the spectre of a global conspiracy seriously. A herald of the apocalypse that was to convulse Lodz Jewry arrived in the early 1930s in the city in the shape of German economist Peter-Heinz Seraphim. Seraphim sought to appraise the assets of a territory that, he believed, might become part of the German Reich in the near future. In 1937 he published the first result of his work: an atlas entitled *Polen und seine Wirtschaft* (*Poland and its Economy*). The book contained maps supplying demographical information, including three that tried to visualize Jewish dominance in the Polish cities (see p. 22). In an accompanying text, Seraphim explained to his German readership that the Polish Jews were very different from the *Assimilationsjuden* (assimilation-Jews) in Western Europe. He stated that, unlike the *Assimilationsjuden*, Polish Jews lived as compact groups, and that in the last century they had left the villages to move to large towns and cities, where they controlled trade, became financiers with a great influence on the economy, "penetrated into" many industries, and had a significant role as industrial entrepreneurs. He added, "Finally: significant for the cohesion of the Jews in Poland is the appearance of a perfectly voluntary *Ghettobildung* [ghetto-formation] in the cities that can be observed everywhere. The Jew, who also stands in sharp contrast to the Christian population by means of the way they are dressed and their traditional hairstyle, flock together in particular neighborhoods where the Jewish population, partly extraordinarily poor and proletarianized, congeals." These were mostly found in the old city centres, and no Polish city showed this better than "the Jewish *Riesenstadt* [giant city] of Lodz." As to the question of why, Seraphim offered a simple answer: "The inner motivation of this voluntary ghettoization is the desire to maintain [demographic] cohesion."[8]

Having become interested in the Jewish Question as it manifested itself in Poland, Seraphim decided to make it the focus of what was to become and remain his magnum opus: the 736-page *Das Judentum im osteuropäischen Raum* (*Jewry in East-European Space*).[9] Richly illustrated with photos and many maps and diagrams and supported by a lengthy bibliography and many footnotes, this publication looked scholarly enough. But Seraphim used facts selectively to support what was a pernicious piece of Nazi propaganda. In the larger towns and the cities, "the ghetto is *the protective wall for the preservation of Judaism,*" Seraphim explained. While he appreciated the legitimacy of this concept in pre-modern conditions, he considered the Jewish-generated ghetto an anomaly in modern times. This made the situation in Lodz interesting, as its ghetto developed only in the nineteenth century and did not have a pre-modern precedent. "Nevertheless one observes especially in Lodz a concentration of Jews in the district of the so-called Old City," he wrote. For Seraphim, the reason was simple: the ghetto was not only a traditional means of defence, but also "the basis of expansion of the metropolitanized Jewry, because the ghetto contains *a concentrated, economic power* that seeks the Judaization of the whole of the urban economy."[10]

Seraphim illustrated this with a case study of the way Jews, moving from their original stronghold in the Old Town and Bałuty, had taken over the New Town, the economic and social centre of Lodz. Two maps summarized the argument graphically. The result, Seraphim argued, was an urban catastrophe: wherever Jews became the majority, neighbourhoods turned into overcrowded and diseased slums. Seraphim argued that Jews took over what had been created by others without adding anything significant themselves: "Perhaps this sterility of Jews from the urban and architectural point of view also resulted from the fact that *der Jude* wished to penetrate into the city as inconspicuously as possible," he wrote. "Therefore they often hide specific Jewish community buildings, such as prayer halls, yeshivas, etc. in the remote corners and backyards of the Jewish ghettos."[11] Obviously, Seraphim had failed to see the abundant and very conspicuous architectural contributions made to Lodz by *Lodzermenschen* like Izrael Poznański, and also to notice the many beautiful buildings that crowded Piotrkowska Street designed by Jewish architects like Dawid Lande and Gustaw Landau-Gutenteger.

In his last chapter, Seraphim contrasted the beliefs of traditional Polish anti-Semitism with the revolutionary insights of Nazi racial anti-Semitism. Stressing the importance of the understanding that Jews were an alien race that could not be assimilated and that sought world domination, he argued for "their removal from public and economic life. Religious conversion cannot change a Jew into a non-Jew, because not the religious, but the hereditary element is the determining factor." Seraphim lamented that Eastern European anti-Semites had insufficiently recognized these facts. They simply "*lacked a uniformly aligned Weltanschauung that grasps the Jews as a racially determined group*, and which demands towards them a *very special* posture. East-European anti-Semitism is largely the result of *economic rivalry*, mixed with emotional and religious-moral opposition. But goals that are nationalistic or inimical to minorities are not yet a *Weltanschauung* and cannot, therefore, have the decisive thrust of one."[12] The last clause clearly suggests the core obligation that came with a *Weltanschauung*: a *Weltanschauung* transcended mere ideology because it not only offered a coherent interpretation of the world, but also provided one that encompassed both the material and the spiritual in a truly cosmic scope. Because of this, the champions of a *Weltanschauung* were not only justified *but even compelled* to demand a total commitment on the part of those who accepted its truth.[13]

Seraphim described the ghetto as a base from which the Jew ventured out into the world. It was a place that was beyond the reach and understanding of non-Jews. It is not clear to what extent Seraphim's book had been on the desks of the Nazi leaders who, in the wake of the November pogrom, also known as "Kristallnacht," assembled in Hermann Göring's office on November 12, 1938. The chief of the *Sicherheitsdienst* or SD (Security Service), Reinhard Heydrich, reminded the gathering about the success of his operation in Vienna, which since the Anschluss of Austria in March 1938 had been able to push Jews into emigration. If such an organization were established in the rest of the German Reich, he believed he might be able to "export" 10,000 Jews each year. "That would leave a great many Jews here. Because of Aryanization and other restrictions Jewry will be unemployed. We will see the remaining Jews becoming proletarians. I would have to take measures in Germany to isolate the Jews, on the one hand, so that they will not enter into the normal life of the Germans." When Göring responded that this would lead to the creation of large ghettos, Heydrich energetically responded that this was unacceptable: "From a police point of view I think that a ghetto, in the form of a completely segregated district with only Jews, is not possible. We would have no control over a ghetto where the Jew gets together with the whole of his Jewish tribe. It would be a permanent hideout for criminals and first of all [a source] of epidemics and the like."[14] Indeed: in late 1938, the Nazi leadership was in agreement that the sole tool to solve the Jewish Question was emigration—voluntary or forced.

To push a largely middle-class and upper-middle-class community that had been extraordinarily successful in economic and cultural terms into voluntary emigration had proven difficult. The philosopher Hans Meyerhof, who found himself a refugee in the United States, reflected in 1941 on why it had been difficult for Jews to leave, even when opportunities existed. "The Jews, except for the Zionists—and they were a minority—had no program for the future, neither for themselves as Jews, nor for their fellowmen as Germans, Austrians, or French," he wrote. "Their program consisted in the preservation of the *status quo*; for only in the *status quo* were security and social prestige.... Thus they remained, until they were driven out; they hung on to their pseudo-security, until nothing could be salvaged out of what they had built."[15] Another German Jewish refugee, physician Martin Gumpert, also reflected on this in that same, crucial year of 1941—the year the Nazi persecution of the Jews turned into the Holocaust: "Emigration represents a break and an impact fortunately realized by but a few. In the middle-class sense it represents a bankruptcy, a degradation: unless one happens to be an Einstein, one is deprived of all one's marks of rank and left only with the opportunity to regain them under completely changed circumstances." Gumpert admitted that leaving one's homeland to begin again overseas might appeal to adventurers. "But we are not adventurers," he confessed. "We are doctors and businessmen with readily checked inventories."[16]

Yet both Meyerhof and Gumpert had more or less voluntarily left before all opportunities ceased. They had made the right calculation and found that there was no future for Jews in Germany, and that the reversal of the emancipation project was permanent. In 1927, the Austrian Jewish writer Joseph Roth had written a long essay about the *Ostjuden* and the alleged *Ostjudenfrage*. In his introduction, he had admitted he did not expect the book to be read by "those 'objective' readers who peer down with a cheap and sour benevolence from the rickety towers of their Western civilization upon the near East and its inhabitants; who, out of sheer humanity, are struck with pity at inadequate sewage systems, and whose fear of contagion leads them to lock up poor immigrants in tenements where social problems are solved by simple epidemics. This book does not want to be read by those who would seek to deny their own fathers or forefathers if they happened to escape from such tenements." Instead, he sought a readership among those who did not look down on the *Ostjuden*: "readers with respect for pain, for human greatness, and for the squalor that everywhere accompanies misery; West Europeans who are not merely proud of their clean mattresses. These are readers who feel they might have something to learn from the East, and who have perhaps already sensed that great people and great ideas—great but also useful (to them)—have come from Galicia, Russia, Lithuania, and Romania." Roth tried to create understanding for the *Ostjude*, who looked to the west as utopia realized. He wrote, "The Eastern Jew in his homeland knows nothing of the social injustice of the West; nothing of the habitual bias that governs the actions, decisions, and opinions of the average West European; ... nothing of the sheer hatred that, like a life-prolonging (though lethal) drug, is so powerful that it is tended like a sort of

Eternal Flame, at which these selfish people and nations warm themselves. The Eastern Jew looks to the West with longing that it really doesn't merit. To the Eastern Jew, the West signifies freedom, justice, civilization, and the possibility to work and develop his talents."[17] As is clear from these introductory words, Roth had looked beyond the modern, cosmopolitian facade of Weimar Germany and seen the narrow horizons and hatred that was to bring Nazism to power.

Living in exile since 1933, Roth planned a second edition of *Juden auf Wanderschaft* (*The Wandering Jews*), and in 1937 wrote a new foreword for the book, which, sadly, was not to appear again until 1985. He observed that, four years after the Nazis had come to power in Germany, the title of the book applied not only to the condition of the *Ostjude*, but even more to that of a new Jewish type, the *Westjude* (western Jew)—the German Jew who, only a decade earlier, had felt himself primarily a German, and on high holidays perhaps also a Jewish German, but who now was also forced from his home. "Some of them unfortunately gave in to the temptation to blame Jewish immigrants from the east for the expression of anti-Semitic feeling. It is an often-ignored fact that Jews, too, are capable of anti-Semitism. One does not want to be reminded by some recent arrival from Lodz of one's own grandfather from Posen or Katowice." Roth identified this as the attitude of the petit bourgeois who is busy climbing a steep social ladder: "At the sight of a cousin from Lodz, one might easily lose one's balance and fall." Yet after four years of National Socialist rule, the German Jew had discovered that he was "more exposed and more homeless than his cousin from Lodz had been a few years before."[18]

Things turned worse a year after Roth wrote these words. By the spring of 1938, it was clear to Nazi policymakers that the attempt to solve the Jewish Question through voluntary emigration had been, by and large, a failure. Thus they began to experiment in recently annexed Austria with a policy of forced emigration, which was overseen by Heydrich and perfected by his specialist in Jewish matters, Adolf Eichmann. Yet even the most well-planned system to strip Jews of their livelihoods and possessions and to provide them with passports and one-way tickets out of the country was dependent on the willingness of other countries to accept the Jews. And in the second half of the 1930s, there was no such willingness. "They pleaded at the consulates and almost always in vain, for which country wanted newcomers who had been plundered to the skin, beggars?" the Austrian Jewish writer Stefan Zweig observed in 1941.

Even the lucky ones, who had been able to leave Germany to find temporary refuge in other European countries, were told to move on. But to where? Zweig, who had left the continent when this was still possible, and who was somewhat protected by his fame, looked with compassion on his fellow Jews as they sought a country that would take them in:

> I will never forget the sight which once met me in a London travel bureau; it was filled with refugees, almost all Jews, every one of them wanting to go—anywhere. Merely to another country, anywhere, into the polar ice or the scorching sands of Sahara, only away, only on because, their transit visa having expired, they had to go on, on with wife and child to new stars, to a new language-world, to folk whom they did not know and who did not want to receive them. There I met a once very wealthy industrialist from Vienna, who had been one of our most intelligent art collectors; he was so old, so grey, so weary that I did not recognize him at first. Weakly with both hands, he clung to the table. I asked him where he was going. "I don't know," he said, "who asks about one's wishes nowadays? One goes wherever one is still admitted. Someone told me that I might be able to get a visa for Haiti or San Domingo here." My heart skipped a beat: an old worn-out man with children and grandchildren, atremble with the hope of going to a country which hitherto he would not have been able to find on the map, there only to beg his way through and again be a stranger and purposeless! Someone next to him asked in eager desperation how one could get to Shanghai; he had heard that the Chinese were still admitting refugees. There they crowded, erstwhile university professors, bankers, merchants, landed proprietors, musicians; each ready to drag the miserable ruins of his existence over earth and oceans anywhere, to do and suffer anything, only away, away from Europe, only away! It was a ghostly flock.[19]

A policy to solve the Jewish Question by means of emigration was only possible if countries were willing to take Jewish immigrants, and only viable as long as trains continued to cross frontiers and passenger ships continued to plow the oceans—in short, it was only an option as long as peace prevailed. By the beginning of 1939, destinations for Jews willing to leave the Greater German Reich— that is, the state that consisted of the German Reich within the borders established at Versailles, former Austria (annexed March 1938), the Sudetenland (October 1938) and the Protectorate of Bohemia and Moravia (March 1939)—were in increasingly short supply, and Great Britain and France were increasingly determined to resist further German demands for territorial revisions. Europe was drifting toward war.

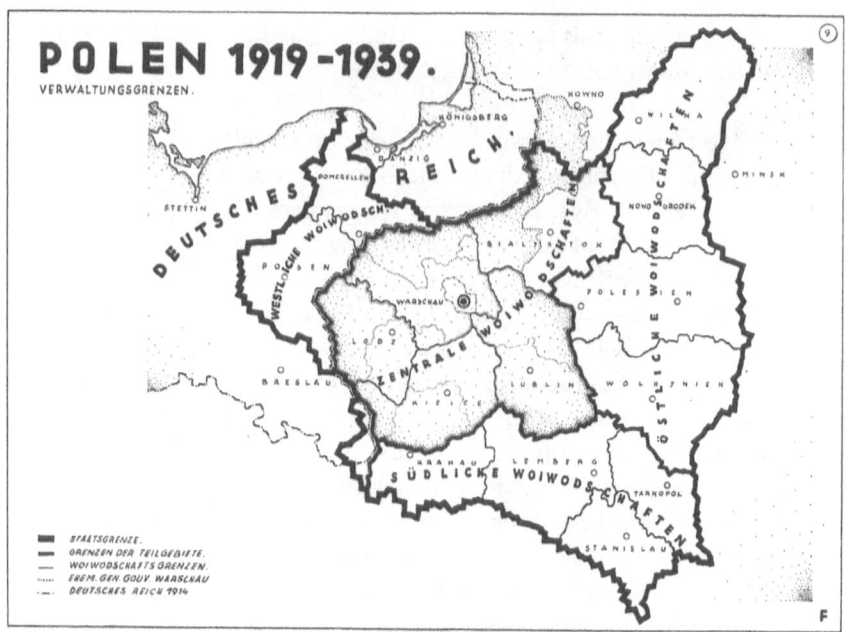

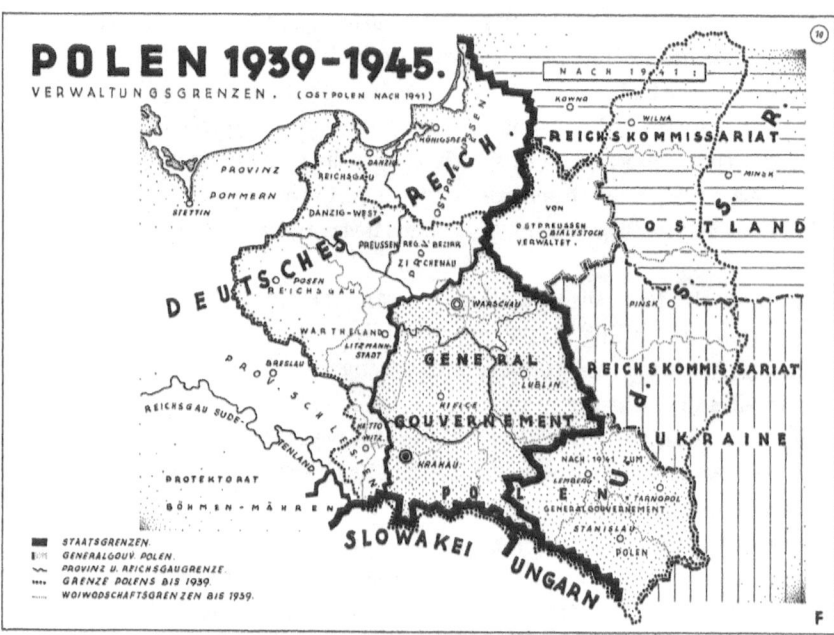

Maps of Poland 1919–1939 and 1939–1945, by Peter-Heinz Seraphim.
Collection of the author.

CHAPTER THREE
Lodz Becomes, Once Again, a German City

On September 1, 1939, the German *Wehrmacht* (armed forces) crossed the German-Polish frontier. A week later, Lodz came under German occupation, and on September 13 Hitler was driven into the city, receiving from ecstatic Germans a hero's welcome. On September 17, the Red Army invaded Poland from the east in accordance with a secret protocol of the Molotov-Ribbentrop Pact, concluded in August. On October 6, the last remnants of the Polish Army on Polish territory surrendered, and Germany and the Soviet Union conducted the Fourth Partition of Poland. There are many maps that try to visualize the complexity of the deal. For the sake of consistency, it makes sense to use the one that Seraphim included in the second and radically revised edition of his economic atlas of Poland, published in 1953.

Seraphim's plate 10 (opposite, bottom) is a complex map that befits a complex historical reality. A heavy black line marks the official border between the German Reich (including the annexed and occupied Polish territories) and the Soviet Union (including the annexed Polish territories) established in the fall of 1939, and the border with Hungary and Slovakia established in early 1939. To the left and right of the black line is a dotted area, named "Generalgouvernement Polen" ("General Government Poland"). The part of the General Government left of the black line is the German-occupied Polish "homeland" as it existed from the fall of 1939 to the summer of 1941, while the part of the General Government right of the black line represents the part added to that "homeland" after the German invasion of the Soviet Union in June 1941. To the left of the General Government is the Deutsches-Reich (German Reich). It consists of an area that belonged to the German Reich before September 1939—commonly referred to as the "Altreich" ("Old Reich"), established after World War I, to which were added Austria (March 1938), the Sudeten area (October 1938) and the Memel territory (March 1939)—as well as the Free State of Danzig and the Polish areas that were officially incorporated in the German Reich in October 1939. These areas, called *"Reichsgaue"* ("Reich provinces"), are Danzig-West-Preussen, Regierungs Bezirk Zichenau (located in Provinz Ostpreussen), the eastern part of Provinz Schlesien and Reichsgau Wartheland. The map shows that the bulk of the Wartheland consisted of a Polish *voivodeship* (province) that had as its capital the city the Poles knew as "Poznań" and the Germans as "Posen." This was, by and large, the territory that had belonged to the German Reich until 1918, and that had been incorporated into Poland in 1919. Plate 10 also shows within the Wartheland, but outside the former Poznań province, a city named "Litzmannstadt"—which is Lodz after its renaming in April 1940. The map reveals a key fact: between the fall of 1939 and early 1945, Lodz officially belonged to the (Greater) German Reich.[1]

When, after the conquest of Poland, German officials began to consider which parts of the country would be occupied and which parts would be incorporated into the Reich, they originally assumed that only those parts lost in 1919—Danzig, the so-called Polish corridor separating East Prussia from the rest of Germany, the province of Posen, and eastern Upper Silesia—would be annexed in a restoration of the status quo ante 1919. As Lodz had not been part of the German Reich before 1919, it was to be part of the General Government. And this made sense: the great majority of the population consisted of Poles and Jews, and the Germans were not interested in including more Poles or Jews within the Reich. Thus, when on October 26 Germany annexed the territories lost in 1919, Lodz was not included.

But the German residents of Lodz desired to see their home become part of the Reich, and they petitioned Reichsführer-SS Heinrich Himmler, Propaganda Minister Joseph Goebbels and Interior Minister Wilhelm Frick when these officials visited the city a few days later. Furthermore, Arthur Greiser, who was appointed *Gauleiter* (Provincial Leader) and *Reichsstatthalter* (Reich Governor) of the Wartheland, desired to provide his largely rural satrapy, centred on the Posen region, with an industrial base. On November 4, 1939, Hitler decided to move the border between the German Reich and the General Government eastward: Lodz was to be part of the Wartheland—but only just. The official incorporation of Lodz within the Reich followed five days later.

Lodz was now separated from half of its rural hinterland and from Piotrków Trybunalski, the place on which it had depended until the 1830s (now known again by its German name, "Petrikau"). The city was thus to have an uneasy location at the eastern border of the German Reich. Economic and regional planners shook their heads: Hitler was, of course infallible, but the precise location of the new frontier did not make any sense. Only one individual had the guts to protest (in a most indirect manner, of course). In 1941, Walter Christaller, who had been commissioned by Himmler to draw up plans for reconfiguring Poland, published an internal document in which he proposed the separation of Lodz from the Wartheland and the creation of a new province that centred on Lodz and reached northward to Włocławek on the Vistula, westward to Koło, southward beyond Częstochowa, and eastward beyond Rawa Mazowiecka.[2] His suggestions were not heeded.

After the final borders of the Wartheland (or the "Warthegau," as it was also known) had been settled, the Germans could take stock. Only 325,000 inhabitants—one out of fourteen of the five-million-strong population—were German. With that small minority as a basis, Greiser and his aides aimed to transform the Wartheland, with the help of Himmler's SS, into "a blonde province."[3] How to achieve a rapid Germanization of a largely Polish territory that also counted 435,000 Jews, more than half of whom lived in Lodz? The answer was simple: create an inventory of the Germans present in the Wartheland that would distinguish them according to levels of commitment to the German cause and ethnic-racial purity; allow willing Poles of "racially valuable" appearance and suspected Germanic ancestry to become ethnic German on probation; settle ethnic Germans from the Baltic countries in the Wartheland; and expel most Poles and all Jews to the General Government.[4] These policies were framed by a general directive, articulated by Heydrich in a meeting held on September 27, 1939, that was attended by the commanders of the *Einsatzgruppen* (Deployment Groups) and department heads of the *Sicherheitsdienst* or SD (Security Service) and the *Sicherheitspolizei* or SiPo (Security Police), including the Gestapo official responsible for Jewish affairs: Eichmann.

Heydrich explained the new territorial arrangements. "At the moment, development in the former Poland is intended to occur in such a way that the former German provinces will become German *Gaue*, and in addition a *Gau* with a non-German-speaking population will be created with Kraków as the capital."[5] The latter area, which was to include also Warsaw, Radom and Lublin, was to become known as the General Government. Teachers, clergy, aristocrats, members of veteran groups and officers living in the annexed territories were to be immediately expelled to the non-German-speaking *Gau*, while the lower classes were to be allowed to remain as seasonal workers for the time being. Heydrich presented a draconian program that clearly violated the Hague Convention of 1907, which stipulated that the occupying power was a trustee of the occupied area until a peace treaty settled its final fate. Obviously the duty to protect life and property, guaranteed by the Polish constitution that the German Army was obliged to maintain, was not relevant to Heydrich. By the time of the meeting, the Polish population in the territories that were to be annexed was effectively outlawed: mass arrests and public executions had become the new normal. In the area that became the Wartheland, this terrorization happened with Greiser's full support: terror, he hoped, would motivate the Polish inhabitants of the territory to leave for the General Government.

If Heydrich and Greiser had no use for the Poles, they had even less use for the Jews.[6] Yet, at least initially, Goebbels was happy to exploit the cinematographic potential of the Jews of Lodz. Nazi anti-Semitism was based on the fiction of a global conspiracy. To transform this fiction into empirical reality, the Nazis were committed to making, whenever and wherever possible, *der Jude* visible. They knew from Kossmann and Seraphim that the occupation of Lodz offered a perfect opportunity to do so—that is, before the expected expulsion began. Immediately after the German conquest of the city, German cameramen from the national weekly news show shown in cinemas, *Die deutsche Wochenschau* (*The German Weekly Review*), began to document Jewish life in Lodz as a manifestation of a mortal threat to Germany.[7] A film crew led by documentary filmmaker Fritz Hippler followed them. They were to shoot scenes for a documentary about *das Weltjudentum* that was to be Goebbels's key contribution to the solution of the Jewish Question.

Hippler's men, backed by the army, filmed mainly in the Old Town. They focused on the filthy appearance of the crowded, impoverished neighbourhood and on particularly unappetizing examples of the Jewish population. They also filmed selected aspects of Jewish ritual life: ignoring completely the many charitable institutions within the Jewish community, they spent much time in butcher shops and slaughterhouses. On October 17, Hippler showed thirty minutes of rushes to Goebbels, including scenes of Jewish ritual slaughter of cows, calves and sheep. "One shudders at such barbarism," Goebbels jotted down in his diary. There was only one conclusion: *"Dieses Judentum muß vernichtet werden"* ("This Jewry must be annihilated"). On October 28, Goebbels showed these rushes to Hitler and his dinner guests. According to his diary, all were "deeply shocked." The footage motivated Goebbels to travel to Lodz to observe *der Jude* firsthand. *"Lodz selbst ist eine scheußliche Stadt"* ("Lodz itself is a hideous city"), Goebbels noted down upon his arrival. "Car-trip through the ghetto. We get out and have a close look at everything. One cannot describe it. They are no longer human beings, but animals. It is, therefore, also no humanitarian task, but a task for the surgeon. One has to cut here, and one must do so in a most radical manner. Or Europe will vanish one day due to the Jewish disease." On his return to Berlin, he discussed his observations with Hitler, and in his diary entry of November 2 he wrote, "Above all my description of the Jewish problem finds his total approval. The Jew is garbage. Rather a clinical than a social matter."[8]

Goebbels and Hitler remained closely involved with the movie, and their ideological guidance and the "talent" of director Hippler, writer Eberhard Tauber and composer Franz Friedl ensured that the result became what British director Laurence Rees rightly characterized as "the most appalling film ever made."[9] On November 20, 1940, *Der Ewige Jude* (*The Eternal Jew*) had its first public showing in Berlin. "The civilized Jews which we know from Germany only give an incomplete picture of their racial nature," it pronounced right at the beginning. "This film shows original footage from the Polish ghettos. It shows Jews as they really look, before they hide themselves behind the mask of the civilized European."[10]

After explaining that the Germans had a first look at the Jewish ghettos in Poland during the Great War, the narrator noted that Germans now had to learn to truly "see" Jews: "Unlike in 1914, we no longer see just the most grotesque and comical of these questionable ghetto figures. This time we recognize that there is a plague here, a plague that threatens the health of the Aryan peoples." Showing slum-like, bug-infested dwellings, the narrator claimed that the inhabitants were wealthy, but preferred to live this way: in other words, the overcrowded slum was the natural habitat of *der Jude*. After mapping the way the Jews had moved from the Middle East to Western Europe, to then settle in the Polish ghettos before advancing to the New World, *Der Ewige Jude* came to its key statement, illustrated by a dramatic juxtaposition between close-up shots of a pack of rats emerging from the sewers and footage of a crowd of Jews moving in the narrow streets of the Old Town of Lodz: "Parallel to these Jewish wanderings throughout the world is the migration of a similarly restless animal: the rat. . . . They are cunning, cowardly, and cruel, and usually appear in massive hordes. They represent the element of sneakiness and subterranean destruction among animals—just as the Jews do among Mankind."[11]

Unlike rats, however, Jews were able to hide their true essence, by assimilation. A number of before-and-after scenes showed groups of Lodz Jews first dressed in traditional garb with beards and sidelocks, and then freshly shorn and shaven and dressed in business suits. These montages proved the Jews were ready to infiltrate the "Aryan" world: they appeared the same as anyone else. *Ostjuden* had transformed themselves into *Westjuden*. "People without good instincts let themselves be deceived by this mimicry, and consider Jews the same as they are," the film's narrator explained. "Therein lies the enormous danger: these assimilated Jews remain forever foreign bodies in the organisms of their host peoples regardless of appearances." The final scene of the movie showed the response Hitler had given to the threat on January 30, 1939: *"Wenn es dem internationalen Finanzjudentum in und außerhalb Europas gelingen sollte, die Völker noch einmal in einen Weltkrieg zu stürzen, dann wird das Ergebnis nicht der Sieg des Judentums sein, sondern die Vernichtung der jüdischen Rasse in Europa!"* ("If the international finance-Jewry inside and outside Europe should succeed in plunging the nations into a world war yet again, then the outcome will not be the victory of Jewry, but rather the annihilation of the Jewish race in Europe!").[12]

The critics got the message—at least about the need to unmask *der Jude* however and wherever he may appear. Journalist Heinz Schwaibold summarized the core idea of the movie in a lengthy review: "The most essential task of this movie is to reveal the sharpest contradiction one can imagine." This was the contradiction behind the civilized mask of World-Jewry and its bestial core. The film's purpose was "to pull the mask from the face of this wolf in sheep's clothes and to also show every German comrade: this is the way they really look, these parasites of humanity! They come from there, from the sewers of the ghetto, from the pestilential bubo of Europe!"[13] And the cinema-going public got the message. On January 20, 1941, the SD reported that public response to *Der Ewige Jude* had been positive, and that viewers had especially appreciated these juxtapositions: "From many conversations we have learned that the contrasting presentations of Jews from all corners of the world have made it abundantly clear that the Jew, despite all apparent adaptation to states, languages, and lifestyles, always remains a Jew."[14]

Seventy-five years after *Der Ewige Jude* was made, it is difficult to imagine it actually had an impact. But its effect lingered in postwar Germany. In 1948, when most Germans had learned to keep their mouths shut or utter pious generalities when foreigners asked them about the German solution to the Jewish Question that had ended in the murder of six million human beings, an architect from Frankfurt am Main spoke candidly to the American sociologist Everett C. Hughes:

The architect: "I am ashamed for my people whenever I think of it. But we didn't know about it. We only learned about all that later. You must remember the pressure we were under; we had to join the party. We had to keep our mouths shut and do as we were told. It was a terrible pressure. Still I am ashamed. But you see, we had lost our colonies, and our national honor was hurt. And these Nazis exploited that feeling. And the Jews, they *were* a problem. They came from the east. You should see them in Poland; the lowest class of people, full of lice, dirty and poor, running about in their ghettos in filthy caftans. They came here, and got rich by unbelievable methods after the first war. They occupied all the good places. Why, they were in proportion of ten to one in medicine and law and government posts!"

At this point the architect hesitated and looked confused. He continued: "Where was I? It is the poor food. You see what misery we are in here, Herr Professor. It often happens that I forget what I was talking about. Where was I now? I have completely forgotten."

(His confusion was, I believe, not at all feigned. Many Germans said they suffered losses of memory such as this, and laid it to their lack of food.)

I said firmly: "You were talking about loss of national honor and how the Jews had got hold of everything."

The architect: "Oh, yes! That was it! Well, of course that was no way to settle the Jewish problem. But there *was* a problem and it had to be settled some way."[15]

This statement by the architect is interesting because it refers both to the imagery shown in *Der Ewige Jude* and to the alleged invasion of the *Ostjuden* after World War I as if nothing had happened since then: the boycott of 1933, the Nuremberg Laws, the November pogrom, the ghettos, the killing squads, the camps with their gas chambers and Auschwitz.

Once the Old Town of Lodz and Bałuty had served as the stages for *Der Ewige Jude*, and the Jews of Lodz as involuntary and unpaid actors, the liquidation of Jewish Lodz—which had begun within days of the occupation with arbitrary harassment, restrictions on the amount of cash Jews could possess or withdraw and forced labour—began to move into high gear. On October 13, the Germans ordered the creation of a *Judenrat*, which was to enforce German policies within the Jewish community. Most of the leaders of the Jewish community had fled to the east. A few weeks earlier, sixty-two-year-old Mordechai Chaim Rumkowski (1877–1944) had stepped into the vacuum as a self-appointed representative of the Lodz Jews, and the Germans decided to confirm his position by giving him the dignity of *Judenälteste* (Elder of the Jews) and charging him with finding thirty-one other members for the council.

Rumkowski was a failed industrialist: before World War I he had owned a small factory that made velvet fabrics, but the business had gone bankrupt. Since then, he had made a living by working as an insurance broker and running the Helenówek orphanage. In his personality and his way of engaging the world, he was a classic example of the *Lodzermensch*. As such, to many he appeared as a blast from the past: energetic bordering on aggressive; capable bordering on domineering; *Fabriken* (willing to take risks); *Wildwest* (hungry for public recognition); and *Provinz* (intolerant and quite vulgar). Rumkowski believed that the occupation gave him an opportunity to make good after a life in the shadows.

Decree after decree, alternated by bursts of lethal violence, rained on the Lodz Jews. On October 18, they were forbidden to trade in leather and textiles, which eliminated the livelihood of a significant part of the population. The next day, a trustee office was established that energetically began to expropriate Jewish-owned factories. On October 31, Jewish shops, workshops and professional offices were marked (which led to systematic pillage by Germans), Jewish employees in all non-Jewish enterprises were fired, and Jewish organizations were forbidden. Jews were also banned from Piotrkowska Street—renamed "Adolf-Hitler Street"—forbidden to marry non-Jews, subjected to a curfew, and forced to wear first yellow armbands on their right arms and then yellow Stars of David on all garments, front and back. On November 10, one day after Lodz officially became part of the Greater German Reich, the Germans burned the four major synagogues in the city.[16]

The next day, at a rally in Lodz, Greiser declared: "Yesterday, during a tour through certain parts of the city, I had the opportunity to encounter figures who can scarcely be credited with the designation 'person' [*Mensch*] and that are still present in much too great a number. In their faces live criminal instincts that stamp them as individuals of the fifth or sixth order. For us, and this I can assure you, the Jewish Question is no longer a problem, even when it confronts us in massed form, like here. It's only for us to solve, and it will be solved."[17] If anyone had any doubt as to the Germans' commitment to solving the Jewish Question violently, the execution of twenty and the arrest of the remaining eleven members of the *Judenrat* appointed a month earlier by Rumkowski made it clear: no one was immune. Rumkowski, beaten on November 11, was spared the gallows or imprisonment. He certainly got the message. He proved to be totally compliant from that day onward.

In November, Greiser expected he could just drive the Wartheland Jews over the nearby border into the General Government. At the time, Himmler, who had been charged in October with overseeing the "ethnic cleansing" of the annexed territories—including the Wartheland—instructed his subordinate Eichmann to set up a Jewish reservation in the eastern part of the General

Government, in the region around the town of Nisko in Poland's Lublin district.[18] The Jewish Question appeared to be more in need of a quick solution in Vienna than elsewhere: deportations of Austrian Jews to Lublin began within weeks. As nothing had been prepared to house and feed the deportees, many died from starvation and disease. The Germans shrugged at the high mortality, but they were convinced by the German Army to stop the deportations: Lublin was to be the staging area for the expected war with the Soviet Union, and the generals did not want to expose their soldiers to the risk of epidemic diseases that, as anti-Semitic propaganda had made clear, were carried by *der Jude*. In the spring of 1940 the project to concentrate Europe's Jews in the Lublin reservation collapsed.

In the meeting on September 27, 1939, Heydrich had sketched the broad lines of the fate of the Jews. He had referred to what became the Lublin reservation: "The Führer has granted permission for deportation of Jews into the non-German-speaking *Gau* [and for] expulsion beyond the line of demarcation [separating German- and Soviet-occupied Poland]. But the whole process should be spread over the duration of a year." This meant that there was a need for an interim solution, and Heydrich used very particular language to introduce the first step: "*Das Judentum ist in den Städten im Ghetto zusammenzufassen um eine bessere Kontrollmöglichkeit und später Abschubmöglichkeit zu haben*" ("Jewry is to be concentrated in the cities in the ghetto to allow for better means of control and a better means of expulsion at a later time").[19] It is interesting that, in comparison with November 1938, he had changed his view on the use of ghettos as a tool of anti-Jewish policy: in the immediate aftermath of the November pogrom, he had resisted the creation of such places in the German Reich because he would not be able to control them. Now, he supported the temporary concentration of Jews "in the ghetto" as a means of control. The difference between the conditions in 1938 Germany and 1939 Poland was, of course, that "the ghetto" was, as Seraphim had shown, a key fact of urban life in the Polish lands.

It is important to note that Heydrich did *not* order that Jewry be concentrated "in ghettos"; he referred to "the ghetto" in the singular. Historian Dan Michman has observed that Heydrich's terminology reveals he did not propose establishing new ghettos in cities, but instead aimed at "*concentrating* and *collecting* or *containing* (*zusammenfassen*) the Jews in existing ghettos." Michman concludes: "It is important to emphasize here that, conceptually speaking, the ghettos were not an *ex nihilo* creation, because ghettos, as the Germans understood them, already existed and were the hallmark of Eastern European Jewry. The Germans merely took the step to demarcate their boundaries and force

Jews who had left them to infect the rest of the city, to return to their 'natural habitat.'"[20] In other words, Heydrich aimed to undo the phenomenon described in the preceding decade by Kossmann and Seraphim and graphically represented in *Der Ewige Jude*, which at the time of the meeting was being filmed in Lodz. By forcing the Jews back into the original ghetto, Heydrich sought not only to create conditions that allowed the Germans to easily contain, control and deport them, as he specifically articulated, but also to achieve a goal he did not articulate in the meeting—one that was central to Nazi anti-Semitism: he forced individual Jews to become visible again as *der Jude*.

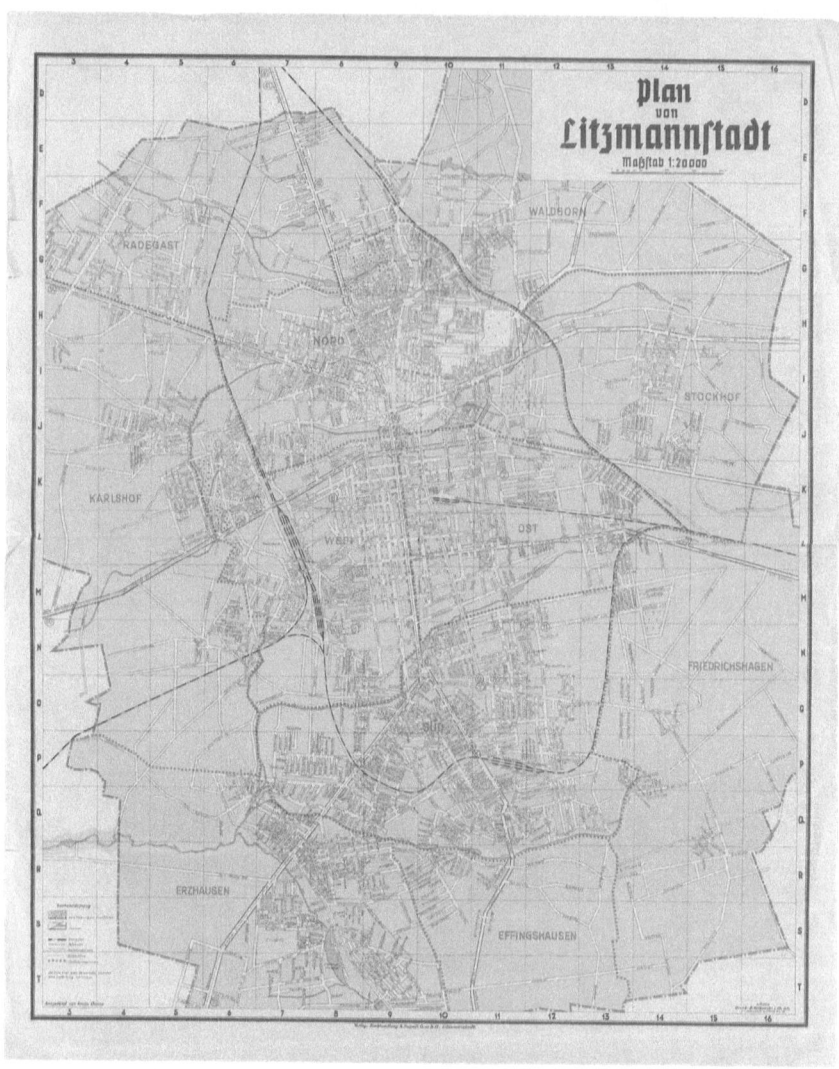

Map of Litzmannstadt (Lodz), Poland, by Erwin Thiem.
The Lodz Ghetto is indicated in white in the upper centre of the map.
Collection Staatsbibliothek Berlin.

44

CHAPTER FOUR
The Starry Sky of Lodz

In December 1939, the German *Regierungsprädident* (Regional Government President) of the *Regierungsbezirk* (region) that included Lodz, Friedrich Uebelhoer, drafted a plan for a closed ghetto in Lodz. It was, as he explicitly stated, a temporary solution, and not all Jews were to be confined to the ghetto, which was to be located in the Old Town. The ghetto was to house those living in the area and those Jews living in the New Town who were incapable of work. Jews living in the New Town who were deemed capable of work were not to be assembled in labour camps. The ghetto was to be maintained on a simple barter principle: food and fuel would be delivered to the ghetto in exchange for textiles and valuables. "In this manner we will succeed in completely extracting the most concealed material assets hidden by Jews," Uebelhoer predicted.[1]

In the months that followed, the plan evolved: the ghetto was to include all Jews. In the meantime, the Germans worked to create a justification for their actions by invoking health concerns. "Due to nasty conditions in regard to hygiene, the north of the city of Lodz, particularly the part inhabited virtually exclusively by Jews, is a constant focus of infection," the German-language *Lodscher Zeitung* (*Lodz Paper*) announced on January 9, 1940. The area was supposedly rife with typhus, typhoid fever and dysentery, and hence "every unnecessary contact with this part of the city must be avoided."[2] A month later, the *Lodscher Zeitung* published an order of the German police chief of Lodz ordering the creation of an official ghetto in the Old Town and Bałuty. It was a literal interpretation of Heydrich's command that the Jews be concentrated "in the ghetto."

The Old Town and Bałuty had been, until 1862, the Jewish district of Lodz, accommodating by the early 1860s some 6,000 inhabitants. By the 1930s, these two districts had become overcrowded slums housing around 60,000 mostly Jewish residents. "Infamous even in Lodz, Bałuty recalls in its architectural image the old town in its lack of space, air, and light," Kossmann had written in 1932. Its tenements, many built from wood, were blackened by smoke. Everything was dirty. Kossmann went on: "Filth can be described as the dominant element that ties everything harmoniously together. The apartments are frighteningly small. The courtyards are filled with caricatures of dwellings and reduced to narrow shafts that bring neither light nor air to the labyrinth of houses."[3] Now the 140,000 Jews who lived in the New Town were to join these impoverished Jews in a fenced- and walled-off area that measured about four kilometres. One-third of the ghetto area was not densely built up: the area of Marysin was to provide the only relief from the slum-like conditions of the Old Town and Bałuty. (That is, if one can take the enormous cemetery that occupied a significant part of Marysin as a source of relief. The late Sholem Aleichem might have thought this possible: in his story "The Town of the Little People," the cemetery is a source of pride and delight to the local Jewish community.[4]) Each of the Jews expelled to the ghetto was allowed to take "basically one suitcase with their linens, personal clothing, and family keepsakes (family pictures and the like), but in quantity such that each individual can carry it without special means of transport."[5]

Within days, a mass movement of people began: small groups of Polish and German residents left the designated area with all of their possessions and with the help of trucks and wagons, and large groups of Jews, almost completely stripped of their belongings, walked in, either carrying a bag or two or pushing a hastily constructed sled through the snow. The *Lodscher Zeitung* celebrated the return of the Jews to their original habitat: "The Jew, who crawled out of the dark corners of the ghetto into the surrounding German neighborhoods and gnawed at the body of the nation, like maggots in meat, has been tamed. He has been sent back to the place he came from."[6] Not all obeyed. From early March onward, the German Army conducted raids in the New Town, evicting those who had not yet moved out of their apartments and killing those who resisted. By April 11, the day Lodz was renamed "Litzmannstadt," in honour of the general who had won the Battle of Lodz a quarter of a century earlier and who had become an ardent Nazi in the 1920s, most of the Jews had been moved.[7]

The Polish and German populations of Lodz stood by as their Jewish neighbours were dispossessed and imprisoned. There was little the Poles could do: every day, they themselves faced terror and the possibility of expulsion to the General Government, or worse. But the Lodzer Germans did not face immediate danger, and there is no evidence they provided even the most basic form of moral support. They were not only drunk with the new and privileged status they had obtained, but had also rewritten the history of Lodz in such a manner that all the credit for the development of Lodz as an industrial metropolis went to the Germans, while *der Jude* was made responsible for every aspect of the decline of the German community since 1918.

The Lodz German industrialist Karl Weber, manager of the textile firm Karl Steinert Aktiengesellschaft (AG) and, since the end of 1939, not only president of the city's Chamber of Commerce but also the German trustee of I.K. Poznański AG, presented this new narrative in an article published in February 1940 in the first issue of a new business magazine published by the Economic Chamber of the Warthegau. After describing the splendid achievement of German entrepreneurs in Lodz, he noted that after 1918 the Polish government had resented the achievement of the Germans, and tried to strangle it by means of taxes and regulations. *"Der Jude proved an ever more dangerous enemy,"* Weber stated. "One can safely state that the history of the Lodzer German economy during the time of Polish rule provides the perhaps most convincing and shocking example of how Jewry penetrates into a completed economical edifice to fragment and destroy it with all means available, and how it makes itself comfortable in all nooks and corners and attempts to devalue, counterfeit and rule every aspect of the life of the city."

Ignoring the achievements of, for example, the Poznańskis—which is odd, as he had been running the Poznański industrial empire since late 1939—Weber described the Jewish attempts to control Lodz before 1918 as doomed to fail. *"The great hour of Jewry came when the Polish state arose,"* Weber stated. Then began *"der Vernichtungskampf*—the war of destruction" against the German community in the city. Completely ignoring the fact that many German entrepreneurs had left the city, and that others had gone bankrupt as the result of the Great Depression, and that Jewish entrepreneurs were the only ones who had been willing to make new beginnings amid the broad economic collapse, Weber described the new businesses established in the ruins of the old manufactures as parasitical organisms that could only grow by exploiting German workers, evading taxes and, when brought to court, bribing judges. The final crime of *der Jude* took place in the spring of 1939, when the (of course) Jewish papers inspired the Poles to begin a reign of terror against the German minority: "It began with the general boycott of all that was German, and ended with mass demolitions, and also with murder and arson; tens of thousands escaped with their naked life by fleeing over the green border in the protective Reich. *The Lodzer German economy stood at the edge of the abyss in the summer of 1939."*[8] This was the propaganda masquerading as history that the Lodzer Germans heard while they saw the arrest and expulsion of their Jewish neighbours.

Greiser's daughter was in Lodz on April 11, 1940—the day the city got its new name. As befitting her status, Irene Greiser received the royal tour, visiting the major sites and engaging in some heavy-duty shopping in warehouses full of confiscated luxuries. "It's really fantastic," she observed after her tour through the ghetto. "A whole city district totally sealed off by a barbed-wire fence." Irene had bought into all the anti-Semitic stereotypes: "You mostly see just riff-raff loafing about. On their clothes, they have to have a yellow Star of David both behind and in front (Daddy's invention, he speaks only about the starry sky of Lodz)." Irene had no illusions about conditions in the place. "In every room there are surely ten to twenty people, I saw so many heads in the windows. There are epidemics here, and terrible air since everything is spilled into the drainage pipes. There is no water, the Jews have to buy it for ten pennies a bucket, and so they surely wash themselves less frequently than usual. Just seeing this can make one sick." Yet she had no sympathy for the ghetto inhabitants: "I think that they feel very differently from us and therefore don't feel this humiliation and everything."[9]

Many more Germans came to visit the ghetto and discover the true face of Jewry. A report on the activities of the district court in Lodz, written in early 1942, proudly noted: "Litzmannstadt possessed as the first German city a closed ghetto and a 'tourist attraction' that never failed to excite the most lively interest of visitors from the Old Reich."[10] The ghetto was represented in the exhibition *Der Osten des Warthelandes* (*The East of the Wartheland*), which opened in Lodz on March 9, 1941, in the presence of Greiser. The show focused on the changes brought about in Lodz since its incorporation into the Reich. In his introduction to the book that accompanied the exhibition, Uebelhoer set the tone: "Everything positive that we encountered in the first November days of 1939 in the chaotic conditions in the East of the Wartheland was created by German diligence and German tenacity."[11]

The book revealed the new self-image of the Germans from Lodz. Gone was the idea that the German, as a *Lodzermensch*, had been an entrepreneur at heart who boldly sought economic opportunities in collaboration with others of a similar mindset, regardless of their ethnic backgrounds or religious affiliations. Now the German community was characterized as a hardened, tightly knit and racially conscious bridgehead of civilization in the chaotic wilds of the east. Not surprisingly, the book buried the contributions of Jews and Poles to the development of Lodz in silence. In the narrative presented, their only role was to obstruct German development and destroy German achievement. Uebelhoer recorded with pride the counter-offensive he had initiated in late 1939, when he had pushed the Jews back to the ghetto from which they had emerged eighty years earlier. "One thing is certain: in Litzmannstadt they have ceased to cheat Germans, they have ceased to steal from them or engage in usury. In Litzmannstadt their reign, which ultimately brings death to every non-Jew, is finally over," he wrote. The propaganda photos taken in the ghetto Uebelhoer had created were captioned by a single sentence, noted earlier, that summarized the Nazi *Weltanschauung* concerning the Jews. Linking the fate of the poorest street urchin in Lodz to the prospects of the wealthiest stockbroker in New York City, Uebelhoer announced: "The vital nerve of International Jewry has been hit in Litzmannstadt."[12]

On April 30, the Germans sealed off what was now officially known as "Getto Litzmannstadt," which I'll refer to in the remainder of this essay as the "Lodz Ghetto." While German tourists could enter under certain conditions, any Jew trying to leave the ghetto without permission—which was rarely given—was to be shot without warning. The Germans and Poles living in the rest of the city were told that "every contact with Jews, also including commercial traffic of the civilian population, is forbidden as of now."[13] This ghetto was a *novum* in history: never before had a ghetto functioned as a permanent prison. Ghettos had been surrounded by boundaries: in the case of the ghetto in Venice, which had given its name to the settlement type, its borders had been marked by canals. (The Venetian noun *"ghetto"* refers to slag, the refuse metal obtained in the process of smelting, and the area Jews had been told to settle was known as "slag" because it had once been the location of ironworks.) In other cases, walls had surrounded Jewish quarters, but the bridges or gates connecting Jews to the rest of the city had been pulled up or closed only at night, and during the day Jews had been free to conduct their business in the non-Jewish part of town, or to leave for other places. The Lodz Ghetto set a new and radical precedent.

The Germans were proud of their achievement. On May 19, 1940, the *Frankfurter Zeitung*, which had been the voice of liberal Germany until the Nazi era, published an article entitled *"Die Juden in Litzmannstadt"* ("The Jews in Litzmannstadt"). It praised the way the ghetto allowed for a radical separation of Jews from non-Jews and kept the Jews isolated in the ghetto. In particular, it marvelled at the ingenuity of making the only place of contact between the ghetto and the rest of the world a goods-loading platform along a railway line located just east of the ghetto, in the Radogoszcz (renamed "Radegast") neighbourhood. "In the ghetto a railway station had been created to serve as a transit point for Jewish production with other products. Food items made available to the Jews are brought to the *Judenhof* [Jewish court] of this transit station, and the Jews have to convey an equivalent in goods to the *Arierhof* [Aryan court] on the other side of the transit station. Officials of the Economic and Food Office determine the exchange value. This means that there is no trade between Jews and Aryans. The goods delivered by the Jews pass through a disinfection chamber."[14]

The Germans established ghettos in ninety-three towns and cities in the annexed parts of Poland, and hundreds in the General Government. All of these ghettos were able to maintain some contact with the surrounding community. Things were radically different in Lodz: for the fifty-two months of the ghetto's existence, it was radically severed from the rest of the city. There are a few explanations for this. The fact that the ghetto was located within the German Reich must have given the municipal authorities extra motivation to ensure that the "contamination" represented by the ghetto remained tightly contained within its walls.

More importantly, Lodz was home to a large, Nazified German population. In Warsaw and other Polish cities and towns, Polish Jews were imprisoned amid Christian Poles. They shared the Polish language and had shared lives as neighbours. And while a majority of Christian Poles was prejudiced against Jews, and a minority was anti-Semitic, few were infected with racial anti-Semitism. Enough Christian Poles realized that the primary enemy was the German and not the Jew, and there was even a minority among them that felt a duty to aid Jews. As a result, the separation between the ghetto and the "Aryan side" of these cities and towns was never absolute. But in Lodz, Nazi ideology had wiped out the reality of whatever past Germans and Jews had shared. As the Jewish presence had been "revealed" as the result of a malicious and covert conquest cloaked in hypocrisy, all the social relations that had existed between individual Germans and individual Jews were retroactively annulled: they had never really existed, as the trusting Germans had been blind to the mimicry of *der Jude*. While Poles remained in Lodz, those living close to the ghetto were all Poles who had been willing to be redefined as ethnic Germans. They had burned their bridges with the rest of the Polish community when they accepted this privileged status, and were bound to go along with whatever the Germans decided to do with the Jews.

On the day the ghetto was sealed off, Franz Schiffer, the German Mayor of Lodz, made Rumkowski fully responsible for the inhabitants of the ghetto. In exchange for this burden, he gave Rumkowski full authority: "I task you with carrying out all measures that are necessary and will be necessary for the maintenance of an orderly social life in the Jews' residential area. In particular, you have to secure the order of economic life, nutrition, labor deployment, public health, and welfare." After informing Rumkowski that all Jewish property had been confiscated, Schiffer authorized him "to engage all Jews for unpaid labor duty."[15] Having been granted total authority, Rumkowski set out to create an effective and absolutely totalitarian administration that, supported by a very efficient police force, penetrated into every last corner of the ghetto by the fall of 1940.

While the ghetto may have tried to offer the appearance of a civic community—albeit a civic community under siege—it missed the essential precondition of a community: pockets of privacy that allowed people to withdraw from it. Under Rumkowski's leadership, the Lodz Ghetto became a totalitarian institution that had more in common with a concentration camp than with any of the other ghettos created in Nazi-ruled Europe. In the Warsaw Ghetto, the *Judenrat* did not seek to control everything. It allowed for the existence of autonomous political, social and cultural organizations, and because of the status of the General Government as an occupied territory, relief organizations from neutral states such as the American Jewish Joint Distribution Committee were allowed some room to operate. Rumkowski did not tolerate any autonomous organizations within the Lodz Ghetto, and as the ghetto was located in the German Reich, foreign relief organizations were not admitted into it. While in the Warsaw Ghetto there was a measure of public space, in the Lodz Ghetto there was none.[16]

The first census, conducted in June, counted 160,320 Jews: fewer than had been expected. It appears that many of the Lodz Jews, realizing that they would have no future in the German Reich and perhaps some future in the General Government, had left to seek shelter with family in Warsaw, Kraków, Kielce and Lublin. Yet 163,320 people were many more than could be accommodated in the Old Town and Bałuty. To make matters worse: the territory assigned to the ghetto was not a single area: the Germans had excluded a major north-south street and also a second east-west street that met this arterial street in the middle of the ghetto area. These streets were bordered on both sides by high walls. The only way for the ghetto inhabitants of the three areas separated by these two streets to communicate was by means of three footbridges that spanned over the walled streets. These bridges acquired an iconic significance, as they were the only places where the ghetto and the rest of Lodz were in visual contact. In Lodz, the bridge, traditionally a symbol of communication, became a symbol of separation. The main connection to the outside world was the Radogoszcz station. This platform was to be the supply point for food and other imports, the arrival point of deportees from the Greater German Reich, and, ultimately, the point of departure for those deported to the death camps.

The Germans were not interested in whether the three-part ghetto they had created provided in spatial terms an *Existenzminimum* (minimum existence) for the 160,320 Jews squeezed within it. In fact, they worked hard to erase the ghetto from their minds and their maps. In 1941, Erwin Thiem created a new map of Litzmannstadt (p. 44). Drawn at 1:20,000 scale, it measured in its published version sixty-nine by eighty-four centimetres.[17] The map depicts the city as a grey surface with streets drawn in white, parks in green and water in blue. Railroads are represented by means of a line of alternating black and white sections. A broken line made of dashes and dots surrounds the grey field that represents the municipality. The grey area is subdivided by dotted lines that mark the boundaries of the eleven districts into which they city was segmented. Interestingly, no line marks the boundary of the ghetto, which is located in the "North" district; the only boundary that truly counted was left out. The ghetto is represented by the absence of the grey tone that characterizes the rest of the city: the blocks are white.

Thiem's decision to use white to represent the ghetto brings to mind Herman Melville's celebrated meditation on the whiteness of the whale Moby Dick: "Though in many natural objects, whiteness refiningly enhances beauty . . . there yet lurks an elusive something in the innermost idea of this hue, which strikes more of panic to the soul than that redness which affrights in blood. This elusive quality it is, which causes the thought of whiteness, when divorced from more kindly associations, and coupled with any object terrible in itself, to heighten that terror to the furthest bounds." Whiteness, Melville argues, is perceived as ghastly and ghostly, as if cursed by an evil spell. One of the many examples he cites for the horror whiteness elicits is the Albino (from the Latin "albus," "white"), a person defined by his or her whiteness. "The Albino is as well made as other men—has no substantive deformity—and yet this mere aspect of all-pervading whiteness makes him more strangely hideous than the ugliest abortion. Why should this be so?" Melville struggled to find an answer, but only came up with other questions. "Is it that by its indefiniteness it shadows forth the heartless voids and immensities of the universe, and thus stabs us from behind with the thought of annihilation, when beholding the white depths of the milky way?"[18] Did any of the inhabitants of Litzmannstadt who bought the map consider the whiteness of the ghetto? It is unlikely.

The Lodz Germans did not care about the ghetto and its appearance, either in reality or on a city plan. Yet they did consider ways to address the chaotic facade of the city itself: as the Germans now claimed exclusive credit for the economic development of Lodz, they also had either to cleverly evade or boldly take responsibility for the way the place looked. Karl Weber took the first approach in an article published in June 1940. "While the industry of Litzmannstadt was at least until the 1880s purely German, the face of the city, as it first presents itself to the visitor, cannot be defined as German," he wrote. "How could this happen? With all the industrial diligence with which Germans pushed the city to its heights, it was because of political reasons never made possible for them to acquire a decisive influence over the government of the city. Here only the Russian or the Pole ruled: and thus it came in the urban form to what Litzmannstadt is today: inconsistently grown, the palace alongside the hut, the factory next to the house."[19]

Karl Marder, Schiffer's successor as mayor, tackled the problem in a different fashion. "One often calls this city the ugliest in Europe, and having done so believes to have characterized its essence," he wrote in the magazine that carried Weber's article. But the city was only ugly when seen superficially. "Anyone who has experienced the city, knows that it has a conquering vitality and rhythm, a captivating creative force and daring, which provides a fanaticism to the work there despite all apparently cultural and civilizational deficiencies." (To Nazis, "fanaticism" carried an unequivocal positive connotation.) For Marder, Lodz was beautiful because of its entrepreneurial soul, which was also hardened by life at both the economic and ethnic frontiers. And it was attractive because Germans like him were resolved to make it into a beautiful city. He listed how in a few months the city had already become more attractive to all who could see it: "The results are in front of all eyes, especially the ordered administration, the ordered food situation, the ordered economy," he wrote. "The appearance of the streets—of course excluding the architecture—can already be called German. Not only in a superficial fashion, because of the street names, the signs, in the way traffic operates, in the encouragingly fast proceeding improvement of facades and shop windows, in the cleanliness of the streets and the care taken of cars, and in the total elimination of the Jews from public life."

According to Marder, the key in the transformation of Lodz from a Polish into a German city was the "already mentioned *segregation of the Jews* in their own, totally closed district. That segregation was the prerequisite for the hygienic, nutritional-economic, ethno-political and ethical rehabilitation of the city." Marder was particularly interested in the *Gettobildun* (formation of the ghetto) because it foreshadowed the future form of Lodz, in which the Germans were to occupy the centre and the remaining Poles the suburbs in the south—in other words, it was a model for dealing with the Polish Question in the future. He added also a final thought on the ethical dimension of what was, at bottom, the incarceration of more than 160,000 men, women and

children in a four-kilometre area of the city: "Ethically the ghetto is significant because it manifests the excretion of an economic thinking that is capable
to destroy the moral foundations of not only the economy, but also culture."[20]

As Marder suggested—but did not fully articulate—the purpose of the
ghetto in the spring of 1940 was fourfold: hygienic, ethical, ethno-political and
economic. As a hygienic measure, it should decrease the risk of epidemics created by the concentration of so many people in such a small area. As an ethical
measure, it should allow for containment of the imagined moral, spiritual and
physical threat emanating from Jewry. As an ethno-political measure, it was
to provide a temporary holding pen for Jews until October 1, which had been
established as the date by which all the Wartheland Jews were to have moved to
the General Government. Finally, as an economic measure, the ghetto offered
the possibility to strip Jews of whatever assets they still had.

The Jews' expulsion to the ghetto had made available tens of thousands apartments and houses, and thousands of businesses were taken over by Germans
without any compensation for their owners. In addition, the ghetto provided a
means to force *der Jude* to give up his hidden wealth: "*Już w podziemiach synagog
wszystko złoto leży*" ("Already a large hoard of gold rests in the synagogue cellars"), Tuwim had written only a few years earlier.[21] The Germans took the sat-
ire seriously: they assumed that the poverty of many Jews who had lived in
Bałuty and the Old Town before the establishment of the ghetto was a ruse, and
that they had great wealth hidden amid the filth. The Germans reckoned that
when food ran out, starvation would motivate the owners of those assumed
riches to barter.

Rumkowski realized that the inhabitants of the ghetto faced catastrophe.
In April, before the ghetto was sealed off, he tried to convince the Germans
that it might be useful for them to capitalize on the considerable labour potential of the many skilled craftsmen among the ghetto inmates. The municipal
authorities were moderately interested, and in May they allowed for limited
production of textiles. Yet they did not want to see large-scale production: they
expected that the ghetto would exist only for a short time, and they did not
want the ghetto to compete for raw materials with the rest of the Lodz factories, potentially creating unemployment for non-Jewish workers. Rumkowski
had one important ally, however: the German Army. As more and more men
were drafted into the armed forces, they needed uniforms, boots and leather
equipment such as saddles for their horses. Traditional suppliers could not keep
up with the demand. The Lodz Ghetto, which included many textile and
leather workers, might take care of the shortfall.

The incarceration of Polish Jews was also designed to make it possible to forget about them If between September 1939 and April 1940 ghettos had served to make *der Jude* visible, by May the war in the west, which led to the invasion and conquest of the Low Countries and France and the Battle of Britain, refocused propaganda on the leaders of the states that held out against Germany: first Winston Churchill, then Josef Stalin, and finally Franklin D. Roosevelt— all hapless puppets controlled by *der Jude*. As Germans were fighting on an increasing number of fronts, Nazi propagandists did not need the Jews of Poland to remind the population of the mortal threat it faced. The daily bulletins from the *Oberkommando der Wehrmacht* (Supreme Command of the Armed Forces), the death notices in the papers, the stories of soldiers on leave and, from 1942 onward, the Allied bombing raids on German cities spoke with a clear language that made the kind of images shot by Hippler's men in Lodz largely irrelevant.

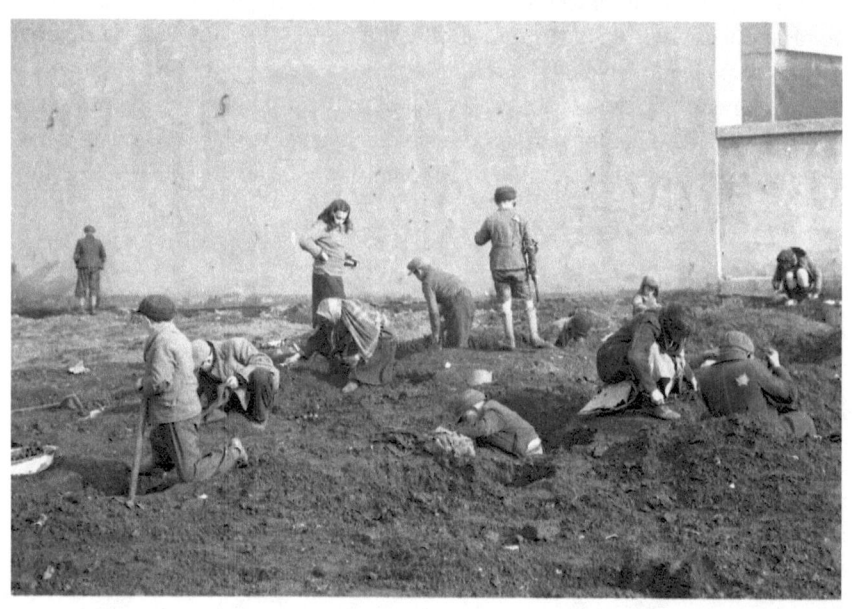

Henryk Ross, *Lodz Ghetto: Children searching the ground for food,*
coal and other provisions, 1940–1944. Print from original 35mm negative.
Collection of the Art Gallery of Ontario, gift from the Archive of
Modern Conflict, 2007. 2007/1999.11.

Deportation Postponed

The conquest of the Low Countries and France in May 1940 led to new speculation on a destination for European Jewry. The Netherlands, Belgium and
France had overseas colonies. In the 1930s, Dutch fascists had called for the
resettlement of Dutch Jews in Surinam, while French fascists had looked at
Madagascar as a dumping ground. In June 1940, Heydrich wrote to German
Foreign Minister Joachim von Ribbentrop that since January 1, 1939, when
he had become responsible for the solution of the Jewish Question, he had
arranged for the emigration of 200,000 Jews. Heydrich complained that the
recent conquests had brought 3.25 million Jews into "areas that are today
under the control of the German state"—by underlining the word "today," he
suggested that tomorrow there might be more. Emigration had ceased to be
a solution: "A territorial final solution has become therefore necessary."[1]
Ribbentrop got the message and set about trying to find a *territoriale Endlösung*
(territorial Final Solution): in the late summer of 1940, the German Foreign
Office adopted the Madagascar option, expecting that France would cede the
island to Germany as part of a peace settlement.

The resulting Madagascar plan taught the Nazis to think big about the
Jewish Question. In the 1930s, they had focused on their mission on getting rid
of all Jews in the Reich; they now sought to free the whole continent from the
"scourge" of the Jews by shipping them to Madagascar. Awaiting the deportation of Polish Jewry to Madagascar, the Germans decided to isolate the Jewish
population in the General Government by establishing closed ghettos that followed the example set in the spring of 1940 in Lodz. While the latter ghetto had
been set up as a very provisional place of confinement in the anticipation of the
deportation of the Jews to the General Government, it now made more sense
to maintain the Lodz Ghetto until the deportations to Madagascar would begin.

In early July, Himmler declared that the expulsion of Jews from the Lodz
Ghetto was unpractical. Greiser was shocked, and on July 31, 1940, he met
Hans Frank, the General Governor of occupied Poland, to see if he could not
find a way to dump the Lodz Jews at some place in the General Government.

He reminded Frank that it had been clear from the beginning that the Lodz Jews would be expelled to the General Government, and that the Wartheland authorities would be unable to maintain the ghetto over the winter. Frank and Bruno Streckenbach, a senior policeman in the General Government, were unwilling to accommodate Greiser, however: they faced a possibility of famine and chaos as things stood. Greiser agreed, and concluded that expulsion was impossible. His aide, Herbert Mehlhorn, made a last attempt to re-open the question. In a lengthy review of the conditions in Lodz he noted that even in the ghetto the Jews could infect Germans who had come from the Reich to transform Lodz into a truly German city and who, unlike the Jews, were not immunized against typhus and other infectious diseases. He concluded that the continued Germanization of Lodz depended on the expulsion of the Jews. Frank shrugged his shoulders. "The *Herr* General Governor recognizes the difficulty of the Jewish problem especially as it concerns Lietzmannstadt [*sic*]," the minutes recorded. "Yet he expressed once again his opinion that the General Government could only offer help once all its food-political and economic problems are solved."[2]

Facing the need to maintain the Lodz Ghetto for at least another year, Greiser began to consider the ghetto's economic potential. Rumkowski's earlier proposals to begin industrial production in the ghetto were now evaluated with greater interest. By this time, the situation in the ghetto was already desperate. Some 70 per cent of ghetto inhabitants had nothing left to barter, and by the end of August food supplies to the ghetto came to a halt. The Germans now faced a choice: either the ghetto was to succumb to hunger and disease or they would have to expend a significant amount of money to feed it: it was estimated that the annual expense to keep the ghetto inmates alive was at least 25 million Reichsmark (RM).[3] Alternatively, the Germans would have to provide an opportunity for the ghetto residents to make a living.

Alexander Palfinger, the second-ranking German in charge of the ghetto, preferred the first option because he believed there were still cash and valuables to be extracted from the imprisoned Jews. In addition, he was an ideological hardliner. "Especially in the Jewish question the National Socialist idea . . . permits no compromise," he stated in a report. "The rapid dying out of the Jews is for us a matter of total indifference, if not to say desirable, as long as the concomitant effects leave the public interest of the German people untouched." Yet Palfinger was also pragmatic, and did not want to risk a fight with Himmler. "Inasmuch, however, as those people in accordance with the instructions of the Reichsführer-SS are to be made to serve the state interest, the most primitive conditions for this must be created."[4] This became the basis of a compromise: the Lodz Jews would be allowed to work in exchange for food in order to maintain their lives at "the most primitive conditions."

In October 1940, Uebelhoer agreed to grant the ghetto a credit of 3 million RM to help it survive the winter. This marked a turning point: from this point on, it was assumed the ghetto would exist for a longer time, and that it would be used as a site for production.[5] The Germans insisted that food would be allocated so that those engaged in production would receive just enough to work (the rations were to be based on those given to Polish convicts), while those not employed—children, elderly people, the ill and others—would receive next to nothing. In other words, in the fall of 1940, the ghetto population was divided into two groups: those who could work and would be fed, and those who couldn't and would starve.

Those who belonged to the large ghetto administration would be fed. And Rumkowski would ensure that some of his collaborators and henchmen and their families were fed very well: all the food supplies coming into the ghetto went through Rumkowski's hands, and he ultimately decided who got what, when, where, why and how. With absolute control, Rumkowski and his apparatus represented what Auschwitz survivor Primo Levi identified as a grey zone of collaboration and privilege amid the general misery. Some may have been terrorized into becoming tools of the Germans, while others were seduced; some may have desired to imitate the powerful, while others may have calmly calculated possible gains and likely losses. All who entered the grey zone desired to preserve a measure of normality in an unprecedented situation. "All these motives," Levi observed, "have come into play in the creation of this gray zone, whose components are bonded together by the wish to preserve and consolidate established privilege vis-à-vis those without privilege."[6]

Now began the transformation of the ghetto from a holding pen into what Litzmannstadt's Mayor Marder characterized as a "*Grossbetrieb sui generis*" ("a unique large company").[7] Run by a German management headed by German businessman Hans Biebow, the ghetto became a massive workshop, a caricature of the industrial city of Lodz that, a century earlier, Germans and Jews had created in what had been in the final analysis a common effort. In early 1941, the official chroniclers of the ghetto wrote with pride about what had been achieved, and in their praise of the new industrial centre created by Rumkowski used language that came straight from Reymont's *The Promised Land*: "The workshops were literally created from nothing. There were no factories, no machines, no appropriate spaces, no grounds, no raw materials and, most importantly, no orders. There was nothing where, today an army of 6,000 tailors...works."[8] Rumkowski: the last and greatest *Lodzermensch!* The German Army, which provided the great bulk of the orders that kept the workshops going, joined in the praise. At the end of 1941, a report on military supplies noted that "under the most severe labor conditions we find here in some sectors surprisingly good results. The Litzmannstadt ghetto with its 170,000 inhabitants has developed in this manner to become the greatest workshop of Germany. ...Their deployment in workshops that are well equipped with machines means, in combination with a way of life at the very lowest level, an enormous possibility to achieve the cheapest production of almost anything."[9]

Indeed, Rumkowski's reinterpretation of Lodz's industrial legacy worked—at least for the ghetto administration and those who had work. *"Unzer Weg is Arbeit!"* ("Our Way Is Work!"), the motto that now guided every aspect of life in the ghetto, was literally true: those who worked got just enough food to survive. At least initially, the workers engaged in strikes to improve their conditions, demanding a bit more money and a piece of bread in addition to the soup served at work. The famous strike of 1905 was engraved in the collective memory of the city as the event that had ennobled Lodz. But if in 1905 the Cossacks had been the tools of suppression, in 1941 it was hunger. Every time a strike began, Rumkowski sat back, withheld rations and waited. Within days, the workers had no choice to go back to avoid death by starvation. On January 30, 1941, Shlomo Frank, a ghetto policeman, wrote in his diary about the end of the strike by the tailors and cabinetmakers: "Great hunger forced them to capitulate. They all returned to work, shaking with hunger. Those who returned had no demands anymore. They did not speak with anyone." In a statement recorded by Frank, the workers explained their decision to go back to work: "We couldn't face anymore seeing our children die from hunger and cold." And they added: "Death to the Jewish traitors! Death to their followers! They will not escape revenge."[10]

The ghetto was a community ruled by the Germans, and by the man often referred to as "King Chaim I." But the most important ruler of the ghetto was hunger. It, more than anything else, destroyed both individual and social bonds. An anonymous girl kept a diary for a few months in 1942, and the focus of almost all of her entries was food, or the lack of it. Often she confessed to her diary that she had taken more than her share of what little food was available to her family. On March 11, 1942, she wrote:

Today I had fight with my father. I swore at him, even cursed him. It happened because yesterday I weighed twenty decagrams [seven ounces] of *zacierki* [dumplings] and then sneaked a spoonful. When my father came back, he immediately noticed that some *zacierki* were missing. My father started yelling at me and he was right. But since the chairman [Rumkowski] gave us these *zacierki* to be cooked, why can't I have some? I became very upset and cursed my father. What have I done? I regret it so much, but it can't be undone. My father is not going to forgive me. How will I ever look him in the eyes? He stood by the window and cried like a baby. Not even a stranger has ever insulted before. The whole family witnessed the incident.[11]

The girl's family belonged to the lucky ones. They had food: too little for life, too much for death. Many people did not have work, and they starved, or, in the winter, froze to death. In his testimony given in Jerusalem, Henryk Ross recalled: "People either swelled up from hunger or became emaciated. There were cases of people collapsing in the street; there were cases where they collapsed at work and at home because of the difficult conditions. . . . I saw entire families, skeletons of people, who during the night were dying with their children. When the neighbours entered in the morning, they saw that all of them had died from frost and starvation."[12]

Between May 1940 and August 1944, when the ghetto was liquidated, 43,725 inhabitants of the ghetto died—more than a quarter of the original 163,777 inhabitants. Of these fatalities, 80 per cent were the direct result of starvation. Residents suffered terrible deaths that had little in common with death in civil society, outside of the ghetto walls. "Death in the Litzmannstadt Ghetto is a strange, unsightly death," the Czech Jewish journalist Oskar Singer jotted down in his diary on July 27, 1942. Singer had been deported to Lodz in the fall of 1941, and never lost sight of the fact that the ghetto was radically different from any other society, even a society under siege. "Here everything is upside down," he noted. "The ghetto was created without any transition, and hence an unbridgeable abyss exists between ourselves and the rest of the world." This was not only because of the physical separation. The ghetto was an elementary catastrophe because it did not offer the possibility of a good and beautiful death; starvation made this impossible. After describing in detail the nature of ubiquitous *Gettokrankheit* (ghetto-disease)—dysentery that triggered an uninterrupted flow of diarrhea that ended in death—Singer concluded his reflection on the perversion of death in Lodz with a short observation: "The doctor writes a death certificate. Cause of death: weakness of the heart! No-one is allowed to die from starvation in the ghetto."[13]

"O Herr, gib jedem seinen eignen Tod. / Das Sterben, das aus jenem Leben geht, / darin er Liebe hatte, Sinn und Not" ("Oh Lord, grant everyone his sovereign death: / a dying extinguishes a life, / which gave him love, significance and death").[14] These lines by the German poet Rainer Maria Rilke were known to the generation of Germans that constructed the Lodz Ghetto. To them, however, *der Jude* did not belong to the "everyone" referred to in Rilke's first line: people who deserved a sovereign death, which means a unique death that is the crown on a unique life. Rilke's lines make clear that Singer touched on a key element in the Nazi assault on the Jews: the fact that the Germans did not consider Jews fellow-mortals. Human beings ought to feel some sense of awe when confronted with the death of another human being—even if this person is a rival, an opponent or an enemy. This awe cannot help but create a solidarity in the face of our common mortality that transcends—in that context *and in that context only*—irrelevant distinctions between perpetrators, victims and bystanders.

Political philosopher Hannah Arendt saw the German concentration camps as places where this violation of our common humanity took place, but she might as well have included the Lodz Ghetto. "The Western world has hitherto, even in its darkest periods, granted the slain enemy the right to be remembered as a self-evident acknowledgment of the fact that we are all men (and *only* men). ... The concentration camps, by making death itself anonymous ... robbed death of the meaning which it had always been possible for it to have," she wrote in an essay on concentration camps. "In a sense they took away the individual's own death, proving that henceforth nothing belonged to him and he belonged to no one. His death merely set a seal on the fact that he had never really existed."[15] The fact that the enemy the Germans were fighting, *der Jude*, was a fiction perhaps explains the German motivation to deny each and every Jew his or her particular death, forcing all of them through that one gate into the hereafter: "weakness of the heart."

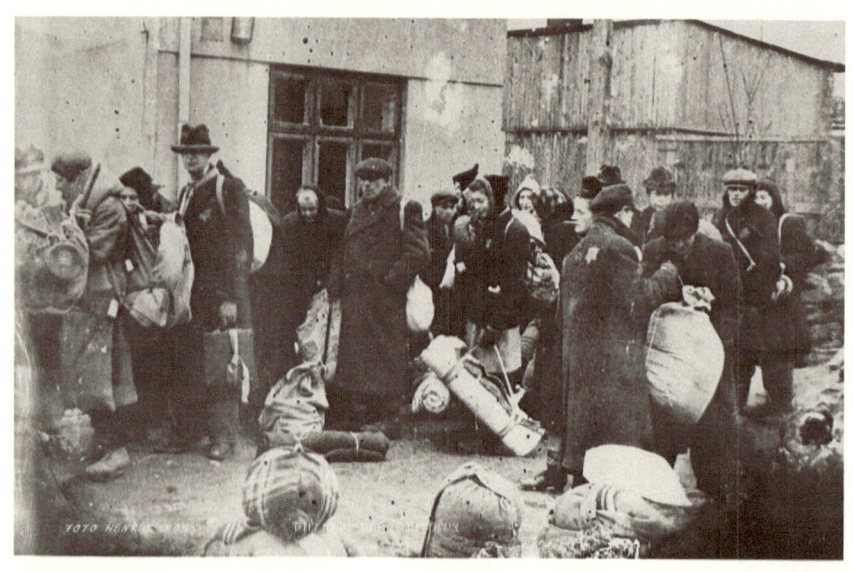

Henryk Ross, *Lodz Ghetto: Residents (with sacks and bedding)*, 1942.
Gelatin silver print from half-tone negative. Collection of the Art Gallery
of Ontario, gift from the Archive of Modern Conflict, 2007. 2007/2640.1.

CHAPTER SIX
Antechamber to Hell

By the beginning of June 1941, all of continental Europe except the remaining neutral countries (Sweden, Switzerland, Spain and Portugal) and the half-Allied Soviet Union was under direct or indirect German control. It was not enough for Hitler. On Sunday, June 22, 1941, the *Wehrmacht* surprised the Soviets with an all-out offensive, an ideological crusade to destroy the Judeo-Bolshevik conspiracy to rule the world. The German invasion of the Soviet Union in June 1941 inaugurated the Holocaust. Killing squads conceived and created by Heydrich followed the advancing *Wehrmacht* to identify, concentrate and execute Communist leaders and Jews. Initially targeting male Jews, the killing squads began murdering all Jews they encountered—men, women and children—in August. The German Army joined forces, and more than 1.3 million people were shot and machine-gunned in the streamlined operation to annihilate Russian Jewry.[1]

As the taboo of the mass killing of women and children was violated in the east, it also became imaginable to consider a genocide of the Jews of Central and Eastern Europe. In July 1941, a senior SS leader in the Wartheland, Rolf-Heinz Höppner, reported to Eichmann—since December 1939 head of RSHA *Referat* (Sub-Department) IV (Gestapo) B (Sects and Churches) 4 (Jews), which was coordinating the anti-Jewish measures—the results of a meeting held in Greiser's office in Posen. "These things sound somewhat fantastic," he wrote, "but I believe they are thoroughly feasible." The key idea was to concentrate all the 300,000 Wartheland Jews in a large camp located in a thinly populated area near the main railway line connecting the mines of Upper Silesia with the harbour of Gdynia, renamed "Gotenhafen" by the Germans. The advantage of a camp over the ghetto was that the Jews would be far away from German civilians, and their risk of causing epidemics would be reduced. "Jews capable of labor may be constituted into labor columns as needed and drawn from the camp," Höppner wrote. The question was what to do with those who could not work. Höppner continued: "This winter there is a danger that not all of the Jews can be fed. One should consider seriously whether it is not the most humane solution to finish off by means of some quick-working substance those Jews who can't be put to work, At any rate, that would be more pleasant than letting them starve to death."[2]

The situation moved from speculation to implementation in the fall of 1941. The plan to concentrate all Wartheland Jews in a single camp never materialized, but the idea to kill those deemed "useless" became a reality. Until the summer of 1941, Hitler had believed that Jews could be used as hostages to ensure that the United States would not enter the war. This assumption was a direct result of his belief that the United States was under the control of *der Jude*, and that it would have some residual concern for the well-being of its original and enduring power base: the Eastern European ghetto as described and analyzed by Seraphim. The United States Congress had already shown support for Great Britain when in March 1941 it approved the Land Lease Act, but a meeting between Churchill and Roosevelt in August 1941, and the resulting Atlantic Charter, made clear that it was only a matter of time before the United States would enter the war on the side of Great Britain, the Soviet Union and the other Allies.

The Jews now lost most of their value as hostages. In early September, it became clear that Lodz was going to be the destination of 60,000 Jews from Greater Germany. Why Lodz? It seems Hitler had decided the Germans Jews were not going to be deported from the Greater German Reich until after the war had finished, and formally Lodz belonged to the German Reich. Between October 16 and November 3, almost 20,000 Jews from Greater Germany arrived in Lodz. If between April 1940 and October 1941 starvation had reduced the population of the Lodz Ghetto from 163,777 to 143,800, the arrival of the transports from the west brought the population back to its original number. In addition, 5,000 Roma and Sinti arrived in the ghetto.

"It is worth mentioning that one result of the resettling of new people here is that the ghetto has acquired an array of talented performers—pianists and singers," a writer employed by the ghetto's Statistics Department noted in the *Biuletyn Kroniki Codziennej* (*The Bulletin of the Daily Chronicle*) in a summary of events that had transpired in November 1941. "The piano performances by maestro [Leopold] Birkenfeld of Vienna deserve special mention. Each of Birkenfeld's concerts is truly a feast for the ghetto's music lovers."[3] Rumkowski realized that the improvement in the cultural offerings in the ghetto was not going to convince the Germans to keep its inhabitants alive, however, and the transports included many who were either too elderly or too young to work.

Rumkowski also feared that the generally highly educated, middle-class Jews from the west would undermine his authority.

The originally Polish Jewish population from Lodz and the German Jewish, Austrian Jewish and Luxembourgian Jewish arrivals were caught in a labyrinth of mutual prejudice. As we have seen, the great majority of German Jews had, until 1933, seen the *Ostjuden* at best as the objects of charity and, from 1933 onward, at worst as representative of their own future. The Nazis had seen them as the true face of every *Westjude*. Until the 1930s, the *Ostjuden* had moved west, and there they had been dependent for longer or shorter times on the goodwill of the *Westjuden*. If Jews from Western Europe had gone east, they had gone as businessmen or tourists or, between 1914 and 1918, soldiers of the German Army. In the east, they may have enjoyed the hospitality of individual Jews or Jewish communities, but they were never dependent on it for their survival. When Jews from the Greater German Reich arrived in the Lodz Ghetto in the fall of 1941, however, they were completely dependent on the existing population: the Germans had made no arrangements for their housing or sustenance, and they had not allowed the deportees to bring anything but suitcases with clothes and a few personal items.

In May and June 1942, Singer subjected what became a unique chapter in the history of the relations between the *Ostjuden* and *Westjuden* to a systematic analysis. He noted that while the Polish Jews in the ghetto certainly harboured a latent hatred toward the German Jews—one that was rooted in the collective memory of the *Ostjuden* since World War I—they initially did their best to receive them "as brothers and sisters."[4] Yet within days, the old prejudices came up. The two groups—those who had been at home in Lodz before the war, knew the place, spoke Polish and/or Yiddish, and learned in two years to negotiate an impossible situation, and those who had just arrived from a totally different life, did not know Lodz, did not speak Polish and/or Yiddish, and were completely unprepared for the human catastrophe they encountered—proved unable to get along. Their relationship collapsed, never to be repaired. According to Singer, when the Lodz Jews heard that *Westjuden* would be brought to the ghetto, they expected a compact, disciplined group of people with a high morale, people who were prepared for a bad situation and would bring to the ghetto a level of organizational skills and technical experience. Instead, the Lodz Jews witnessed the arrival of all those who had been the most vulnerable in their home cities and towns, and who did not have the contacts, resources, energy or cunning to emigrate before this became impossible, or to become considered essential and indispensable when the deportations began. Many of the arrivals were elderly people. A good many had been born *Ostjuden*, moved west during World War I or immediately thereafter, and tried desperately to lose any appearance of their *Ostjüdische* past—a transformation caricaturized in *Der Ewige Jude*. Completely self-identified as German Jews, they were now back where they had come from—except that "where" had turned from a repressed memory into a nightmare.

The *Westjuden* could not take it. Initially, they tried to hang on to shreds of their adopted identity: for example, some refused to exchange the standard yellow star issued in Greater Germany, inscribed with *Jude* and worn on the left breast, for the two uninscribed yellow stars that were standard in the Lodz Ghetto, worn on the right breast and the back.[5] And they looked with astonishment at the *Ostjuden* that surrounded them. "Children lounge around the schools in which we are housed," fifty-eight-year-old Czech journalist Oskar Rosenfeld noted. He had been deported from Prague to Lodz in November 1941, and recorded the first encounter between the *Westjuden*, who, despite all privations, had still lived with basic amenities, and those who had survived sixteen months in the ghetto:

> Deprivation screams from their eyes. Once they get something, they come back again and again—like gypsies who attach themselves to the big hearts that disseminate alms among them. Impossible to get rid of them. Not a flicker of shame left in them. No longer creatures with a soul. They don't speak, they only stare at you. It's impossible to resist the gaze. A gnawing, rumbling in the pit of the stomach, the palate demands to be whetted. You still have an appetite. But here in the eyes of the children you see for the first time in your life the word that had been an empty concept to you and was only known in legend. The word: "Hunger." We used to read: Famine in Russia, in China millions died of hunger... newspaper headlines, sensations for indulged European readers. Now, at last, in its brutal, inescapable nakedness: Hunger![6]

The arrivals were in a state of utter shock. First of all, they had not yet recovered from the deportation itself, during which they were reduced from a people who had lived in cities and towns they knew well, in apartments that offered some measure of comfort and independence, amid their own belongings, to a people robbed of everything except the clothes they were wearing and a few personal items. After a rough trip, they found themselves in a filthy, crowded ghetto amid people whose language they did not speak. Then they experienced the shock of being allocated to terribly overcrowded dormitories erected in former schools, filthy places without beds and often also without bunks, without bed linens or blankets, without light and without running water. Few of the deportees were prepared for this: they were unable to keep themselves or their surroundings clean, and they were put on minimal rations as no one had any work—Rumkowski had decided that only those speaking Yiddish and Polish could be employed in the administration. The mass quarters soon became dens of contagion and turned into dying pens.

As they declined and died in their quarters, the deportees did not become the focus of charity. To the contrary: they became the focus of official censure. The only way for them to get some extra food was to sell whatever belongings they had been able to take along, and this created a black market with an inflation that enraged Rumkowski. "Profiteering is mushrooming," he told the Lodz Jews in his New Year's speech given on January 3, 1942. "As I have stressed many times before, the newcomers are leading a life that is simply unforgivably frivolous. They still suffer from the mistaken belief that the present situation is already coming to an end and, under influence of that delusion, are living from hand to mouth, selling off everything that they brought here with them. Unfortunately, the present situation will go on and on .... Given that, reason would suggest the necessity of spending one's money as cautiously as possible." Rumkowski made it immediately clear that the German Jews could not count on any special help that might give them some incentive not to trade in their belongings for some extra food. "It will be a bad day when the newcomers need to start receiving relief. It is out of the question for me to institute special relief programs for them .... Before the transports arrived in the ghetto, I had succeeded in eradicating parasitic trade in food," he said.[7] In other words, the arrival of the *Westjuden* marked for Rumkowski a defeat, and he proved unwilling to "forgive" them for this.

Singer noted that a number of deportees did not suffer silently: from the moment they arrived in the ghetto, they criticized whatever they encountered. Wherever German Jewish refugees had found refuge after 1933, they were commonly identified as the *"bei unser"* ("by us people"), as they had a habit of always comparing their current situation with their old positions and possessions: *"bei uns in Deutschland war alles besser"* ("by us in Germany everything was better"). This applied not only to their personal circumstances, but also to public life: anecdotal evidence suggests that the typical German Jewish refugee of a certain age could not resist the urge to compare the sloppy discipline of the average soldier in his or her country of refuge to the splendid posture of the German recruit.

In the 1930s, Dutch, English and American neighbours could shrug their shoulders when they encountered such misguided chauvinism, but an inmate of the Lodz Ghetto who had already suffered for two years the dubious benefits of German superiority had little reason to laugh it off. Singer observed that many German Jews loudly offered their opinions on the terrible conditions in the ghetto, crediting it to the backwardness of the *Ostjuden* and not to the conditions created by the Germans. Some of them immediately approached Rumkowski, offering their expertise in order to set things right and turn Lodz into a model ghetto. "Well, the ghetto was already organized," Singer wryly observed, "and better than the German Jew understood, because he had no idea of the difficulties and the grotesque circumstances that made it almost impossible to create even a halfway tolerable coexistence within this community. No, the Chairman [Rumkowski] did not need German Jews to organize the place. He needed, however, fresh labour to undertake work, and such labour did not come forward: the people had fallen too suddenly and too deeply, and proved unable to recover in a short time."[8] As a result, the German-speaking Jews who had been sent from various places in Greater Germany to the Lodz Ghetto in the fall of 1941 did not become integrated into the community. For the local population, they became the object of some anecdotes illustrating the naiveté of *Westjuden* in general, and for the rest they remained objects of general indifference. In a situation of a continually unfolding catastrophe, this boded disaster.

Would things have been different if both the old residents of the ghetto and the new arrivals from the west had cared more deeply about the other side? Would it have been different if Rumkowski had shown leadership in embracing the *Westjuden*, and if the latter had elected leaders who would have been able to help them negotiate the situation? It is unlikely. Looking at the history of the Holocaust as a whole, one can safely say the Nazi persecution, which targeted first the German Jews, then the Austrian, Czech and Polish Jews, to finally engulf the great majority of European Jews, did not provide a crucible in which the myriad life forms of European Jewry could be forged into a single community: this would only happen in Eretz Israel, when these different groups would become involved in a common project to build a new nation—and even there it proved difficult enough, with prejudices between German Jews and Polish Jews, and between European and Middle Eastern Jews, persisting for decades.

But to return to the 1940s: the inability of the *Westjuden* and *Ostjuden* to bridge their differences in Lodz was the expression of a general inability of European Jews—traditionally a collection of very fractured communities—to unite in the face of the Nazi and then the German onslaught.

When Hitler came to power, Jews were separated by nationality, language, religion, levels of religious observance, culture, social class, political affiliation and so on. In other words, whatever they were, they were exactly *not* what the Nazis claimed they were: a single, unified racial body that acted with a single purpose. As we have seen, the Nazis worked hard to transform all these individual Jews into *der Jude*, but although their attempt may have convinced those who flocked to the cinemas to watch *Der Ewige Jude*, it did not produce unity among the victims of Nazi anti-Semitism. "Misery acquaints a man with strange bedfellows,"[9] Trinculo declares in Shakespeare's *The Tempest*, but this has never meant the strange bedfellow becomes a trusted companion. Many who were affected by the Holocaust later reflected on the fact they saw no evidence that the shared experience of persecution brought Jews of different backgrounds together. In fact, a majority agreed that the reverse was normally the case.

Döblin, who had visited Lodz in 1924, fled Germany in March 1933 to become in the years that followed an astute observer of refugee life. In 1939, he travelled by ship to New York to address the PEN Club, and noted the lack of a sense of common destiny among the Jewish refugees onboard. "And now they are on the ship, and they can speak and talk—for the first time in many years they can talk freely. But few do it. . . . One is silent, one is unable to speak, and one chooses not to speak, yes to even know." Locked into their own experiences, the refugees had no sense of a common destiny. "What struck me so much, and here not for the first time, but already in 1933 in Paris, was that while these expellees all talked about that they had been expelled not because they had committed a crime, but simply because they were Jews, that nevertheless beyond that no sense of communality arose between them. Everyone was isolated, private, and remained so. The whole was interpreted as a blow by fate, and that was where it remained."[10]

On this trip, Döblin travelled to the United States as a regular passenger with a visa and a return ticket. A year later, he found himself a refugee in a long line-up before the French consulate in Marseilles in the wake of the German conquest of France. In this line, he met many he knew, and they all speculated about whether the Nazis would come after each of them specifically, or whether they were doomed to suffer an anonymous fate. "There exists among us exiles no solidarity," he later wrote. "We had always led very private lives; now we were particularly isolated from one another. We saw each other at the consulate and nodded: 'Ah, you're here, too,' but no one revealed his plans or the names of those on whom he depended. We guarded secrets. We were distrustful and feared that others would turn to them also, and steal our place."[11]

Döblin was lucky: a famous writer with good connections in the United States, he received a U.S. visa and found safety. In 1942, the German Jewish journalist Theodor Wolff, who had fled to France in 1933 and had not been able to get out, reflected on the fundamental paradox that had shaped the European Jewish experience since 1933. On one hand, the reason for the persecution was the Nazi assumption that all Jews—young and elderly, rich and poor, capitalist and Communist—were part of a single, worldwide conspiracy: that all Jews formed a single body. "The whole doctrine of race is constructed on the false assumption of solidarity," Wolff noted. He also observed with some sadness that even the governments of democracies that had been until the outbreak of the war countries of refuge went somewhat along with this Nazi assumption: they postulated a Jewish obligation of solidarity by insisting that their own nationals of Jewish descent ought to take care of refugees.[12]

Given such assumptions, Wolff wondered whether the persecuted had solidarity among themselves: "Does refugee existence create new obligations, a comradeship, a sense of collegiality, a stronger bond?" He noted it did not. While they lived in the shadow of the story about ancestors who "marched through the Red Sea, apparently shoulder to shoulder, each in solidarity with the person at their sides," the Jewish victims of Nazi persecution did not live up to the example set by the Israelites. And how could it be different? They spoke different languages and had different backgrounds:

Ought the cultivated, dignified Jew with the highest spiritual and moral values feel any relationship to the cynical, amoral wheeler-dealer without ideals or principles, or to the rude pusher, or the small, half civilized upstart, or to the big businessman who, amidst distress full of hungry people, shows off the money he has recovered from the shipwreck? He did not respect or know of greet them in Berlin, Posen or Vienna. No, one has no solidarity with the immense, confusing mix of people, which wanders in exile through the countries. ... This emigration is not a tightly organized caravan, as were the Huguenots, the French protestants who emigrated after the Revocation of the Edict of Nantes, or like the Englishmen who, escaping the papist Stuarts, journeyed to America on the Mayflower—people who felt united by a similarity of habits, customs, even fashion and appearance, and above all by a unity of ideals and purpose. This emigration is a confused, haphazardly thrown together mass in flight after hastily having left and so different in their characteristics as the great and the small creatures who flee in a panic a prairie-fire.[13]

Wolff noted that the disunity among the victims was unavoidable because the cause of their victimhood was neither a shared political ideology, social class or race, but a fiction. Yet it was a powerful fiction, and a dangerous one, as the assumption that Jews were united appeared to justify holding one group of Jews (in Lodz, for example) hostage to ensure the good behaviour of another group of Jews (in Moscow or New York City, for example). "From the theory of a solidary liability must arise the practice of solidary execution, in the same way as in logic the premise determines the conclusion, and as in tragedy the exposition gives rise to the final catastrophe," he wrote.[14]

This, then, was the larger context of the largely silent and largely hidden drama that unfolded in Lodz in the fall, winter and spring of 1941–1942, when an abyss opened between the Lodz Jews and the German, Austrian and Czech Jews dumped into the ghetto by German decree, and when an abyss opened among the *Westjuden* themselves. As they crowded and starved in what were essentially refugee camps within the ghetto, the *Westjuden* lost their ability to socialize even among themselves. "At the same time, a terrible loneliness spread over the newcomers, despite the cramped quarters," Oskar Rosenfeld noted in his diary in April 1942.

> People from all categories slept, breathed, and vegetated next to each other, strangers to each other despite the common suffering and same prospects for the future. . . . Any kind of intimate life had been squashed, living together became painful . . . families torn apart. . . . Where are my children now? My brother? My friends? My books? And suddenly, despite hunger and cold, out into the cold courtyards, to the frozen boards of the latrines. . . . And suddenly again screams for bread, for water, for potatoes. Yes, slowly it dawned on all of us, the merciless truth of the words with which the brown shirts had described the ghetto of Łódź: *the croaking hole of Europe [der Krepierwinkel Europas]*.[15]

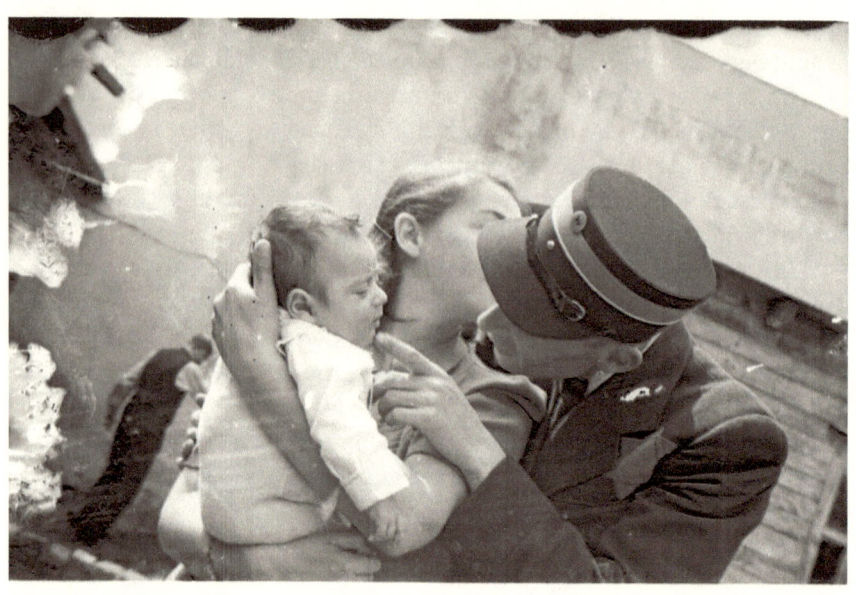

Henryk Ross, *Lodz Ghetto: Jewish policeman's family*, 1940–1942.
Print from original 35mm negative. Collection of the Art Gallery of Ontario,
gift from the Archive of Modern Conflict, 2007. 2007/1988.13.

Holocaust

But for Lodz to become a *Krepierwinkel* for Jews from the Greater German Reich, it had to provide space for them to die. Greiser was appalled by the arrival of the Jews from Greater Germany: from 1939, he had wanted to make the Wartheland *Judenrein* (Jew-free), and now it became a dumping ground for Jews. As the trains with Jewish deportees arrived from the rest of the Greater German Reich at the Radogoszcz station, Greiser made the decision to murder Polish Jews incarcerated in the Lodz Ghetto who could not work—a decision that he knew would not harm his relation with the military. It proved a decisive step in the history of the Holocaust: it was the first time Jews outside the occupied Soviet territories were included as a matter of principle in the unfolding genocide.

Greiser entrusted the operation to the Higher SS and Police Leader in the Wartheland, Wilhelm Koppe, who ordered Herbert Lange to set up a killing installation. Lange commanded a roving, gas van–equipped unit that had been killing inmates of mental asylums since early 1941. Now Lange was to make a pivotal and historic contribution to the Final Solution of the Jewish Question: he conceived of a three-part extermination facility.[1] The first part was a waiting area. A synagogue in the town of Koło (renamed "Warthbrücken"), located some seventy kilometres from Lodz, and an abandoned mill near the village of Zawadki were to function as holding pens for Jews arriving in Koło by train. Lange decided that the second part, a loading station for gas vans, was to be located in the village of Chełmno nad Nerem (renamed "Kulmhof"), located a few miles from Koło. A partly ruined manor house was to serve as the place where the victims would undress, and where they would be tricked to enter gas vans, which would park with their holds pulled up to a crude loading bay that connected to a corridor in the house. The victims, sent down the corridor toward "shower rooms," were to end up in the holds of the vans. Once the spaces were filled, the doors would be closed, and the vans would pull away from the building. Exhaust piped into the hold would do its lethal work. A forest located some five kilometres from the manor house was the third part of the facility: the site of the mass graves. The actual killing was to take place during the drive between the manor house and the forest.

On December 8, 1941, Lange engaged in a first trial of the unprecedented facility. The guinea pigs were Jews from the surrounding area. The production of death proved satisfactory. Four days later, Hitler passed a death sentence on all Jews: they had lost all value as hostages now that Japan had pulled the United States into the war on the Allies' side. Hitler believed that by killing the Jews in Europe he would deal a lethal blow to those in America, and, by implication, to the United States as a whole. In a speech to senior Nazis on December 12, he announced "a clean sweep" to solve the "Jewish Question." Recording this event in his diary, Goebbels noted that in Hitler's speech of January 30, 1939, "he had warned the Jews that if they again unleashed a world war, they would be destroyed. That has proved no empty threat." Paraphrasing Hitler, Goebbels continued, "The world war has arrived, and the destruction of Jewry must follow."[2]

On December 16, Rumkowski heard that 20,000 Jews were to leave the ghetto—exactly the number that had been brought into the ghetto in October and November. An entry in the December 20 *Daily Chronicle* noted: "Through persuasion and request, the Chairman succeeded in having the number of ghetto residents to be resettled reduced by half. The Eldest of the Jews also won permission to decide for himself, on the basis of his authority of the internal autonomy of the ghetto, who is to leave the ghetto." The *Chronicle* noted that it appeared that those who were to leave the ghetto would be sent to the General Government. Recent arrivals were to leave, and also "the so-called undesirable element from the point of view of the ghetto's public interest, including those who are serving sentences and their families."[3] Others whose continued presence was not in the public interest included those receiving welfare, Jews from rural areas who had been recently brought to the ghetto and the Roma and Sinti. Children, the elderly, the sick and the *Westjuden* were to be exempt from deportation. The selection criteria were clearly informed by the wish not to create an uprising in the ghetto, and also by the wish not to offend the Germans, who had explicitly forbidden Rumkowski to include the recently arrived Jews from the Greater German Reich in these deportations.

As Rumkowski and some aides made up the lists of those to be sent out, ghetto production continued. On January 4, 1942, Rumkowski noted in his New Year's speech that he had created "enormous establishments for productive labor" that employed more than 50,000 people. "From the beginning I have been striving to achieve one basic goal. That goal is to be able to demonstrate to the [German] authorities that the ghetto is composed exclusively of working people, that every able-bodied ghetto dweller has his own line of work," he declared. This did not bode well for those who did not work, or who did not do "useful work." In his speech, Rumkowski spoke about the ghetto like a *Lodzermensch* about a plant, and in fact made a direct comparison between the ghetto and the factories that had made Lodz famous: "Last year my monthly balance exceeded three million marks and, of that sum, more than one third was absorbed by social welfare. Financially, I am in much better shape than many of Łódź's important pre-war manufacturers."[4]

In the meantime, preparations for the deportation and killing of tens of thousands of ghetto residents came to a completion. The first group to be dispatched to Chełmno was the Roma and Sinti, followed by Polish Jews. From January 16 to 29, and from February 22 to April 2, the Germans dispatched fifty-four trains carrying 44,076 people from the Radogoszcz station to Koło. These transports did not include the deportees from the Greater German Reich. However, in April, Hitler made the decision that all Jews, irrespective of national origin, were to be included in the genocide, and the ban on including German Jews incarcerated in Lodz was lifted. In the first days of May 1942, Rumkowski decided to include mostly elderly German Jews, who did not have the necessary skills to make uniforms or army equipment, in the trains leaving for Koło. Without roots in the community, their existence in the ghetto had been precarious from the beginning.

To be fair to Rumkowski: he may not have known the fate of those leaving. In mid-April, the *Chronicle* received an entry that relayed information a Gestapo officer had provided about the fate of the deported: they had been sent to a camp. "It has now been irrefutably established that the camp is located in the region bordering directly on the town of Koło, now called Warthbrücken," the article claimed. "The camp houses about 100,000 Jews, indicating that besides the 44,000 resettled from this ghetto, Jews from other cities have been concentrated in that camp. This gigantic camp was formerly a living site for Germans from Volhynia. Apparently 30,000 people had been living there. They left the barracks in perfectly decent order, and even left their furniture for the Jews to use."[5] The story made sense: every inmate in the ghetto knew their fate was tied up in the great demographic changes initiated by Greiser. Germans arriving from elsewhere needed to be housed in transit camps, and it appeared logical that these camps would be reused for the resettlement of Jews. The fact that Koło was only the facade of an extermination facility in Chełmno was unimaginable.

Nevertheless, if the information provided by the unnamed Gestapo officer might have brought some hope to those willing to grasp at straws, the treatment at the Radogoszcz station of the first group of German Jews dispatched to Koło should have made clear that these individuals were doomed. "On May 4, it was off to the station," Rosenfeld recorded in his diary two months later. "Rainy, cool. There the German Kripo [*Kriminalpolizei* or Crime Police] held sway. A wild scene ensued at this first transport. The Kripo took away people's rucksacks and bread sacks. Any kind of foodstuff they carried was taken away. Blankets, pillows, warm clothing. Despair. What to do? Hopeless. Along with it all, whippings for those who weren't able to go fast enough. *Threat of being shot!* Hands up! No-body was allowed to carry anything by hand. Wedding bands surrendered. Watches. Complete beggars." Similar scenes accompanied the transports that followed, removing a total of 12,000 people, mostly *Westjuden*, from the Lodz Ghetto. "The tragedy is immense," Rosenfeld observed. "The tragedy is tremendous. Those in the ghetto cannot comprehend it. For it does not bring out any greatness as in the Middle Ages. This tragedy is devoid of heroes. And why tragedy? Because the pain does not reach out to something human, to a strange heart, but is some-thing incomprehensible, colliding with the cosmos, a natural phenomenon like the creation of the world. Creation would have to start again, with *Berajshit* ["In the beginning," the first word in the Hebrew Bible]. In the beginning God cre-ated the ghetto..."[6]

"Barely half a year has passed since they [the *Westjuden*] arrived in the ghetto," the *Chronicle* recorded on May 7. "At that time they arrived here in long lines, festively-attired people whose appearance contrasted so sharply with our native squalor. We were struck by their elegant sports clothes, their exquisite footwear, their furs, the many variously colored capes the women wore. They often gave the impression of being people on some sort of vacation." In six months, the *Westjuden* had reached the bottom. "Some of the metamorphoses could not be imagined even in a dream. .... Ghosts, skeletons with swollen faces and extremities, ragged and impoverished, they now left for a further journey on which they were not even allowed to take a knapsack."[7]

With the deportation of the German, Austrian, Czech and Luxembourgian Jews to Chełmno, the Germans had crossed the last boundary in the Final Solution of the Jewish Question: if in July 1941 all Jews in the occupied Soviet territories had become outlaws who could be killed as a matter of course, and if in December 1941 the Polish Jews had become outlaws, now every Jew in German-controlled Europe had become a target for murder. True: German Jews had been subject to mass execution in the Riga Ghetto and the Jungfernhof concentration camp in March 1942, but it appears that these killings were the result of local initiatives, and were not coordinated with Berlin. On May 9, 1942, the inclusion of the *Westjuden* in the Holocaust became a matter of policy, with the departure of a train carrying 938 German Jews from Frankfurt am Main to the Sobibór death camp. On June 11, 1942, Eichmann attended a meeting at the offices of RSHA Referat IV B4 in Berlin, in which he informed his deputies in the Hague, Brussels and Paris that they were to organize the immediate deportation to Auschwitz of 15,000 Jews from the Netherlands, 10,000 Jews from Belgium and 100,000 Jews from France. A few days after the meeting, it became clear the Germans would not be able to arrest and transport more than 40,000 Jews from France over the summer: the Vichy government put up a fight to prevent the deportation of French Jews. Eichmann reviewed the situation and increased the number to be deported from the Netherlands from 15,000 to 40,000. Unlike in France, the Netherlands had no collaborationist government to consider.[8]

By the end of May 1942, almost 55,000 inmates of the Lodz Ghetto had been murdered in Chełmno; some 104,500 Jews remained. Over the following summer, the Germans liquidated the remaining Jewish communities in the Wartheland, sending the majority of the Jews to Chełmno, and deporting 14,400 to the Lodz Ghetto. It may seem callous to summarize in a few lines the murder in Chełmno gas vans of more than 100,000 people, the majority of whom came from the Lodz Ghetto. I have chosen not to dwell on heart-rending scenes of families being torn up, on the fear and the terror the victims experienced in their last days and hours, when they were driven to Chełmno, forced to undress and go to the "shower rooms" located at the end of a long corridor. I have chosen not to speculate on the last minutes, when the doors closed, and they began to move, and exhaust fumes began to fill the crowded space, which was now revealed to be the hold of a truck.

When, in early 1945, survivors of the death march from Auschwitz arrived in the Buchenwald concentration camp, they told, in whispers, about the gas chambers of that camp. As he was listening to the testimony given in a darkened barrack housing inmates suffering from contagious diseases—a place that was allegedly safe from SS spies—Jorge Semprun, a veteran of the Spanish Civil War and a man who had seen much death, realized that the gas chambers—sealed places in which people died without witnesses—marked a radical departure in the history of humanity. "The experience of the annihilation of the European Jews has this tragically specific particularity that there are no survivors who can testify," he wrote many years later. "There are no survivors of the gas chambers. No one can tell us that he was there, no one could ever, through the truthfulness of his story, make us say: It is as if I was there!" Throughout history, massacres had been witnessed, if not by victims or bystanders, then certainly by perpetrators. This is why it had always been possible for others, upon hearing their testimony, to think: "It is as if I were there!" Semprun realized that the absolute separation between the inside of the gas chambers and the outside, where the rest of humanity dwelled, made such a thought obscene. "Hundreds of thousands of Jews of all social conditions, all ages, men and women, children and elderly people are dead in the gas chambers, and no one can testify," he wrote. "We have the proofs, but not the testimonies. In humanity's collective memory, legendary or historical, fable or document, there will always be this ontological vacuum, this lack of being, this appalling emptiness, this infected and poisonous wound: no one could ever tell us that he has been there."[9]

We have no testimony of what happened in the wheeled gas chambers at Chełmno, but we have many records of what was, without doubt, the most horrifying period in the history of the Lodz Ghetto: September 1 to 12, 1942. The food situation had worsened over the summer, especially after caterpillars destroyed the cabbage crop produced in the gardens of the Marysin district. These cabbages had been an essential part of the food supply, as very few vegetables had been coming into the ghetto. Starvation became worse. "Pale shadows trudge through the ghetto, with endemic swellings on their legs and faces, people deformed and disfigured," the *Chronicle* reported.[10]

Until this time, Rumkowski had been able to prevent the splitting up of families. The Germans now decided, however, that there was no reason to keep "useless mouths" in the ghetto, and they decreed that those who could not work would be forcefully separated from the rest of the population and sent to Chełmno. Rumkowski was only informed at the very last moment. A month earlier, Adam Czerniaków, head of the Warsaw Ghetto, had faced a similar situation. Unwilling to deliver children to the Germans, he had chosen to commit suicide. Rumkowski made a different decision: he complied.

On September 1, 1942, Rumkowski ordered the Jewish police to surround the hospitals, remove the patients and load them onto trucks bound for the Radogoszcz station. "The morning of the third anniversary of the war was soaked in tears that could not rinse the dust and the blood from the ghetto streets," journalist Jozef Zelkowicz wrote in his diary. "The news—'The sick are being taken from the hospitals'—spread like wildfire across the ghetto. Fearful pandemonium began. Who in the ghetto did not have someone in the hospital? Who did not have a wife, a child, a father, a mother, a relative there?"[11] From all over the ghetto, people ran to the hospitals, but were stopped by lines of policemen. There were no goodbyes.

Three days later, at 2 p.m., notices were posted announcing that Rumkowski was to speak at 3:30 p.m. in Firemen's Square. A crowd gathered, and after more than an hour, Rumkowski appeared. Zelkowicz noted he looked dishevelled and broken. The mighty *Lodzermensch* had lost his gamble: he faced bankruptcy. "A grievous blow has struck the ghetto," Rumkowski told the crowd. "They are asking us to give up the best we possess—the children and the elderly. I was unworthy of having a child of my own, so I gave the best years of my life to children. I've lived and breathed with children, I never imagined I would be forced to deliver this sacrifice to the altar with my own hands. In my old age, I must stretch out my hands and beg: Brothers and sisters! Hand them over to me! Fathers and mothers: Give me your children!" After many such self-pitying words, Rumkowski turned to the facts of the matter:

> They requested 24,000 victims, 3,000 a day for eight days. I succeeded in reducing the number to 20,000, but only on condition that these would be children below the age of ten. Children ten and older are safe. Since the children and the aged together equal only some 13,000 souls, the gap will have to be filled by the sick. I can hardly speak. I am exhausted: I only want to tell you what I am asking of you: Help me carry out this action! I am trembling. I am afraid that others, God forbid, will do it themselves. A broken Jew stands before you. Do not envy me. This is the most difficult of all the orders I've ever had to carry out at any time. I reach out to you with my broken, trembling hands and I beg: Give into my hands the victims, so that we can avoid having further victims, and a population of a hundred thousand Jews can be preserved. So they promised me: if we deliver our victims by ourselves, there will be peace.[12]

Rumkowski faced the nefarious—but, to the Germans, logical—consequence of his offer to make the Lodz Ghetto into the largest workshop in the history of the city: if it were to be a *manufaktura* (workshop), then there was only room for those who could work, for "useful" Jews. Factories—at least the plants created by *Lodzermenschen*—did not maintain playgrounds, hospitals or old-age homes, so the factory overseen by Rumkowski was to get rid of the ballast. Those who were deemed "useless mouths"—the very young, the very elderly and the sick—would have to leave, for the Radogoszcz station and beyond.

The next day, Rumkowski announced a curfew of indefinite duration that would start at 5 p.m. "It has begun," Zelkowicz jotted down in his diary that morning. The streets were filled with masses of people, all silent. "Rigidity, terror, collapse, dread—there are no words to describe the feelings that well in the frozen hearts that cannot cry, cannot even scream.... People hurrying, rushing.

The air laden with oppression; morbid tidings in its weight. The sky constantly swelling and welling, soon to burst and spill out utter horror and utter reality. It has begun!"[13] At 7 p.m., the hunt began—and lasted for seven days. Jewish policemen, supervised by the Germans, searched every building. Henryk Ross, who witnessed it and photographed whatever he could in peril of his life, testified about these days during the Eichmann Trial. "The trucks came to the front of the hospital where the children were assembled," he recalled. "The Germans threw the children from the second floor and from the balconies. The children were of various ages, from one year to approximately ten years. The Germans threw them from the balconies on to these open trucks, on top of the sick people. A few children wept, but most of them were already not crying. The children scratched the walls with their fingernails. The children did not cry any more, they knew what awaited them, they had heard about it. They could not cry."[14]

And then, after seven days, it was over. Almost all who were younger than ten and older than sixty-five—some 15,865 people—and 1,250 hospital patients had been sent to Chełmno. The families of ghetto officials, ghetto police, firefighters and the volunteers who had helped in the search had been exempt from the deportation. To ensure they would not be caught up in the confusion, these families had been brought to a central place where they were safely kept. But ultimately, the whole operation had been a bit more arbitrary than the Germans had intended. "Outward appearance was the deciding factor in obtaining an exemption [of deportation]," the *Chronicle* reported. "It was observable that people who looked better, and particularly those wearing clean clothes, were not taken. There were cases of people over 70 being allowed to remain, while middle-aged and even young people were taken if their appearance betrayed weak health."

The *Chronicle* also noted the surprising attitude of the people: they seemed to immediately forget their terrifying ordeal and grievous losses to focus, once again, on food. "Is this some sort of numbing of the nerves, an indifference, or a symptom of an illness that manifests itself in atrophied emotional reactions? After losing those nearest to them, people talk constantly about rations, potatoes, soup, etc.! It is beyond comprehension."[15] The *Chronicle* reported that women cried for their children, but, as a whole, the ghetto population moved on. "There is little left to talk about: What comes after is only reverberation, echo, a trembling of nerves," Oskar Rosenfeld wrote down some weeks later.

After this experience, our existence, always on the brink of death, has taken on a very simple form, restriction to the absolute necessary. We are alive— some say—because we have reduced our lives to the most primitive level.

We are alive—say others—because we are still keeping alive the sentiments for what's great and just, and that which lies in the future.

We are alive—say some—because everything we do has to serve the preservation of life.

We are alive—say others—because we still have a sense of the metaphysical—We have adjusted ourselves to the present situation, but our inner being is prepared for the future.

In store for us are: rifle, typhoid fever, gallows, death.[16]

By the end of the September 1942, some 90,000 Jews remained in the ghetto. One of the unique characteristics of Jewish religion is the fact that it locates eternity in the continuity of generations: the son is born so that he may bear witness to his father's father. "The grandson renews the name of the forebear. The patriarchs of old call upon their last descendant by his name—which is theirs," the eminent German Jewish religious philosopher Franz Rosenzweig wrote in his *magnum opus* composed in the trenches of World War I. "There is only one community in which such a linked sequence of everlasting life goes from grandfather to grandson, only one which cannot utter the 'we' of its unity without hearing deep within a voice that adds: 'are eternal.'"[17] Because of this collective sense of immortality, located in the everlasting chain of generations, Jews could forego to claim its eternity by means of the possession of land. Yet that very chain was now broken.

The Lodz Ghetto had ceased to be a community: it now became a factory only. On September 21, 1942, the *Chronicle* noted the arrival of large machines from the Radogoszcz station: "A new era is thus commencing in the ghetto: the passage from handicrafts to machine work."[18] Representatives of the German Ghetto Board started visiting the Labour Departments to supervise production and maintain discipline. If much of the production before September had been artisanal in character, the Germans now endeavoured to modernize the existing ghetto workshops and the new ones created in now-empty hospitals, old-age homes and orphanages. This in fact stabilized the situation for the remaining 90,000 inmates, 73,000 of whom were directly involved in production. And as the great industrial cities in the west had become the target of Allied bombers, the industries in the Lodz Ghetto and the surrounding city became increasingly important in German armament production. One consequence of the Allied air raids was the need for emergency homes, and the ghetto developed a prefabricated home that could be produced cheaply in its workshops, shipped to the bombed cities, and erected quickly without the need of skilled labour.[19]

As a measure of stability returned to the ghetto, Ross went around with his camera, photographing the workshops and also the tiny islands where conditions transcended the barest essentials. The most important of these could be found in Marysin, an area located in the northwest of the ghetto. It included the cemetery, some fields, gardens and cottages, and had been, until September 1942, the site of training centres run by Zionist and other youth organizations for Palestine and some twenty kibbutzim. Marysin was also the location of children's camps and a holiday area for the ghetto elite: those involved in the administration, the firefighters and the ghetto police. After September 1942, it was the elite who dominated life in the area. The many photographs Ross made in Marysin show people trying to maintain some measure of normality amid the madness. They show the sons and daughters of the elite celebrating birthday parties in a ghetto without children. They show tables laden with food in a ghetto that hungers. After the war, in Israel, these images were neither exhibited nor published. They did not fit the ideal, projected backward, of a common Jewish solidarity against Nazism. And for those who knew the Nazi discourse on Jews, they fitted all too well the assumption that *der Jude* did not know how to make a community, that he was a greedy profiteer who looked out only for himself, that he was a being without loyalty or solidarity.

Yet one can also consider these images in a different light. For a decade, the Nazis had only been interested in photographing or filming Jews to expose *der ewige Jude* behind each individual. When Ross looked through the viewfinder of his camera, he looked for people, individual people, caught in a terrible and terrifying situation—individuals who made the best of it. His pictures do not invite rage, fear or hatred, but compassion, and a prayer for mercy—for them, for those who placed them in that situation, and for all of us. And they also invite reflection on the fact that each of these people was murdered within weeks, months or perhaps a year after the light that reflected on them hit the emulsion on the film in Ross's camera. We may safely say that each of his pictures was the last record of a unique life.

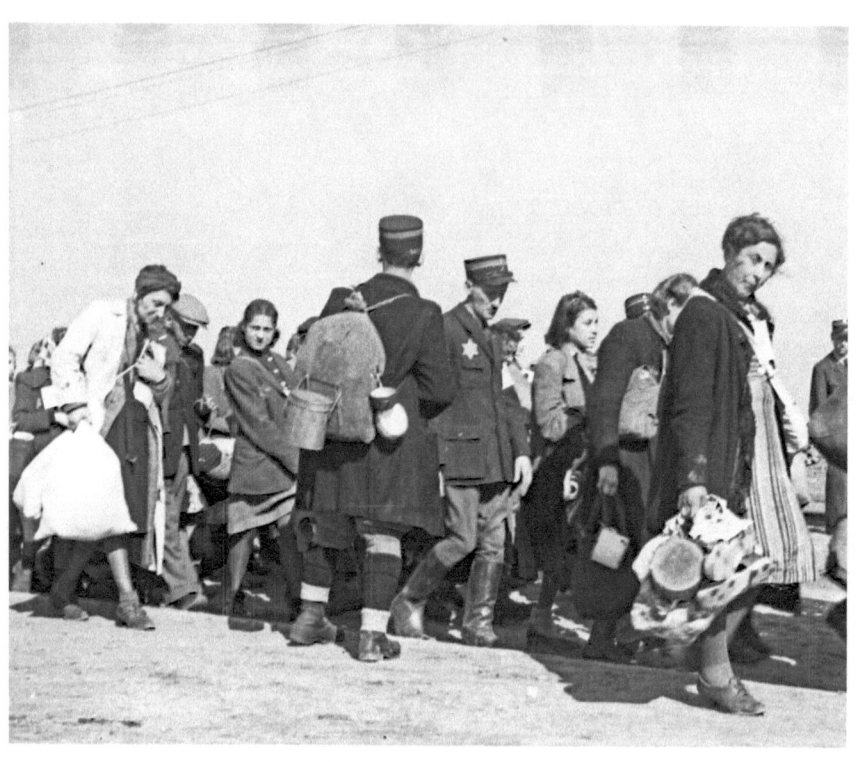

Henryk Ross, *Lodz Ghetto: "...more deportations."* 1944.
Print from original 35mm negative. Collection of the
Art Gallery of Ontario, gift from the Archive of Modern
Conflict, 2007. 2007/1960.4.

The End

Beginning in the spring of 1943, Himmler initiated the liquidation of the remaining ghettos in the east. Concentration camps were to be the only places for Jews. The Warsaw Ghetto Uprising played a significant role in his decision: it had been difficult to suppress, and as the Russian Red Army pushed the German Army back, Himmler did not want to have places full of desperate people willing to follow the example of the Warsaw Jews. Yet he proved unable to close the Lodz Ghetto, as Greiser, supported by the army, successfully resisted him. In September 1943, the Lodz Ghetto thus held the largest group of Jews in German-ruled Europe. It was a group with a broken spirit: unlike the Jews from the Bedzin, Bialystok, Czestachowa, Minsk Mazowiecki, Kraków, Vilna, Warsaw and more than ninety other ghettos, these prisoners had not engaged in an attempt to rise up against their fate. And in the following year, when the Lodz Ghetto was the only major ghetto to remain in existence, they would still not attempt to do so.

There are different explanations for this. Located in the German Reich and in a city with a large German population, the Lodz Ghetto was more radically isolated than other ghettos. In addition, Rumkowski's ghetto administration penetrated the ghetto so ruthlessly and pervasively that there was no space for subversive activity. And the uprisings that had taken place were generally acts of desperation undertaken when the end of the community was imminent. In Lodz, there were always enough glimmers of hope for enough people, as well as enough resentment between the have-nots and the haves, to prevent the emergence of a determined opposition.

In the spring and early summer of 1944, there was hope that the Red Army might soon be at the gates of Lodz. On June 6, 1944, an anonymous boy wrote an English-language entry in his diary: "Today the news of the . . . penetrated into the ghetto. Who knows?" The next day, he added, again in English: "It is true, the fact has been accomplished, but shall we survive? Is it possible to come out of such unimaginable depths, of such unfathomable abysses?" In the days that followed, the boy continued to refer obliquely to what he did not dare name directly: the Allied invasion in Normandy. On June 11: "I go on dreaming, dreaming, about survival and about getting fame, in order to be able to 'tell the world' . . . to tell and 'rebuke,' to 'tell and to protest,' both seems at [the] present moment remote and unbelievable—but who knows maybe, perhaps. I dream to be able about telling humanity but should I be able? Should Shakespeare be able?"[1] As the prospect of liberation increased, he continued to ponder the problem of testimony. On June 14, he wrote: "Man can traverse seas and cross oceans, others fly to the stratosphere, try to reach other planets, but to truly comprehend the suffering of human beings in Litzmannstadt would be an impossible task. The human language is too poor to describe the suffering of Jews in the ghettos of 1944."[2]

The worsening of the German military position in Poland meant a death sentence for the Lodz Ghetto's inhabitants. In the spring of 1944, Himmler decided to liquidate the ghetto. He had various reasons: ethnic Germans fleeing the Red Army were streaming into Lodz, and needed food and supplies. In addition, he feared that upon the approach of the Red Army, the remaining 65,000 ghetto inmates would break out of their prison and take revenge on the 140,000-people-strong German population of Lodz. Even after he had overseen the murder of six million Jews, for Himmler the spectre of the ghetto as a major threat to non-Jews remained alive and well. He thus ordered a resumption of deportations to Chełmno, which had been out of commission for a year and a half.

Between the end of June and the middle of July, ten transports brought more than 7,000 people to Koło to be murdered in Chełmno. On June 24, 1944, the *Chronicle* carried the following entry: "The ghetto is agitated because the railroad cars of yesterday's transport are already back at Radogoszcz station. People infer that the transport only a short distance, and a wave of terror is spreading through the ghetto. People recall the frequent shuttle of transport cars and trains during the period of the great resettlements [of 1942] and the alarming rumors of that time."[3] Yet it also tried to find some silver lining in an unprecedented element of the deportations: the inclusion of skilled workers who were essential for the industrial production of the ghetto. "The consensus of opinion is that the travelers are not headed for any dire fate," the *Chronicle* reported. "They are definitely expected to be employed as laborers and treated humanely. That is why the chairman demands that only the truly healthy and able-bodied be dispatched."[4]

Yet not everyone was fooled: on June 26, the anonymous boy jotted down in his diary: "My friend and I spent a few hours discussing the situation in Chełmno. We shudder with fear and feel, in every bone in our bodies, revulsion towards this accursed 'European civilization,' which elevates itself above others, to a 'moral level.' Woe and woe! to such a level. We all said that at the present moment we cannot feel the depth of the tragedy because all our senses are geared toward the matter of eating."[5] Yet, at the same time, the day-to-day struggle to remain alive was also on his mind. On July 3, he wrote: "I am in a bad mood because I spilled a few grams of flour, because a few slices of my bread were stolen, and ... because the deportations are continuing. In our present situation it is not preposterous to compare the disappearance of bread with deportations, as one and the other could prove fatal to us. It is the best indicator of our unbelievable psychological degradation that in the ghetto people are equally upset by the disappearance of a few bites of bread and by the death of their own father."[6]

There were others who believed the Lodz Jews might just survive to see the defeat of Nazi Germany. Rosenfeld, who had been a skeptic all along, could not suppress an expression of hope. "After five years of war we can finally breath free!" he wrote on July 28. "The word is getting around that we'll soon be redeemed."

> There are plenty of skeptics, nigglers, who don't want to believe it and still have doubts about that for which they have been longing and waiting for years. They are being told: "It has to come sometime, and now that time is here, you don't want to believe it." Then they look with a vacuous gaze into empty space and bask in their pessimism. After so much suffering and terror, after so many disappointments, it is hardly surprising that they are not willing to give themselves over to anticipatory rejoicing. The heart is marred with scars, the brain encrusted with dashed hopes. And if, at long last, the day of the "redemption" should be at the doorstep, it is better to let oneself be surprised than to experience yet another disappointment.[7]

Subsequent events proved the pessimists right. On July 23, 1944, the Red Army had liberated the Majdanek concentration camp near Lublin, and the exposure of the gas chambers and crematoria to a crowd of journalists proved a public relations disaster for Germany in general and the SS in particular. In view of the fast approach of the Red Army, Himmler decided it would be prudent to erase Chełmno from the earth and push ahead with the liquidation of the Lodz Jews.

On August 2, Rumkowski issued the last of his proclamations: "On the instruction of the Mayor of Litzmannstadt, the ghetto will be evacuated. The workshop crews will go as units, together with their families."[8] Having operated as a factory, the Lodz Ghetto was to be liquidated as a factory: plant by plant, workshop by workshop. Biebow, the German manager, directly addressed the workers in the Lodz Ghetto. He had never done so before, and would never do so again. "In this war, in which Germany is fighting for its life, it's necessary to transfer workers to lands from which, at Himmler's orders, thousands of Germans have been taken and sent to the front; they have to be replaced," he declared.[9] Experienced workers—the Lodz Jews—were to be those replacements.

The anonymous boy did not believe the official story: "I write these lines in a terrible state of mind—we have, all of us, to leave the Litz. Getto [sic] during a few days. When I first heard of it I was sure this mean[t] the end of our unheard martyrdom equatanously [together] with our lives, for we were sure that we would be 'vernichtet' [annihilated] in the well known ways of theirs. People were regretting that they didn't die on the first day of the war," he wrote. He was especially disgusted by the response to Biebow's speech. When the manager had asked the crowd if they were willing to work faithfully for the Reich, the Lodz Jews had responded with a "Jawohl—Yes, indeed!" The boy "thought about the abjectness of such a situation! What sort of people are the Germans that they managed to transform us into such low, crawling creatures, as to say 'Jawohl.' Is life really so worthy?"[10]

On August 8, 1944, the first train with workers and their families left the Radogoszcz station. It was headed indeed for a massive plant: the death factory at Auschwitz. Many trains followed. The last train, carrying Rumkowski in a separate carriage—courtesy of Biebow—left on August 31. It is not clear what happened to Rumkowski when he arrived in Auschwitz; there are many competing stories. Some say that at the Rampe (platform) in Auschwitz, the Germans handed him to his fellow deportees from Lodz, who murdered him before being subjected to selection themselves. Others say that Rumkowski was allowed to watch the gassing of the transport of Lodz Jews through a peephole, and was then thrown in the crematoria ovens—alive. And some say he was lined up with all the other men, deemed "useless" by the SS doctor and sent to the gas chambers. As stories, each of the three carries the signature of revenge. And the last one, also the signature of truth: what is certain is that neither Rumkowski nor another 40,000 Lodz Jews survived the day they arrived in Auschwitz.

The rest were admitted to the camp or sent on to other camps. Some survived. About 600 officials of the ghetto administration, engineers, lawyers, doctors and their families were chosen by Biebow for labour deployment in a camp to be built in Königs Wusterhausen near Berlin. A satellite of the Sachsenhausenb concentration camp, Königs Wusterhausen, was to be a construction site for the prefabricated parts of the emergency dwellings developed in the Lodz Ghetto. Mendel Grossmann, who with Ross had recorded the Lodz Ghetto in photographs, was included in this "privileged" transport. He did not survive the war.[11] The Germans had also held back more than 800 Jews in the Lodz Ghetto, including Ross and his wife, to search for remaining valuables and clean the area, making it habitable as temporary shelter for German refugees arriving from the east. On January 19, 1945, the Red Army arrived in Lodz. Most of the Jews, including Ross, were still alive—if only by chance: a few days before the arrival of the Red Army, the Germans had ordered them to dig their own graves, but then fled westward before they could begin the final massacre.

Getto Litzmannstadt Judenpost stamps depicting Mordechai Chaim Rumkowski
and the Zigerska Street bridge, both defining symbols of Lodz, 1940. 7 gelatin silver
prints mounted on card. Collection of the Art Gallery of Ontario, gift from
the Archive of Modern Conflict, 2007. 2007/27.30.

The flight of the Germans concluded the German history of Lodz—one that had begun so promisingly in 1823 to end so ignobly between 1939 and 1945. The onetime German inhabitants joined millions of other German refugees and expellees from the German territories that the Potsdam Conference assigned to Polish and the Soviet "administration" (East Prussia, Danzig-Eest Prussia, Wartheland, Upper Silesia and Lower Silesia) and ethnic German expellees from the rest of Poland, Czechoslovakia, Hungary, Yugoslavia and other countries. They tried to build up a new existence in the Federal Republic of Germany and the German Democratic Republic, united since 1990. Unlike the refugees and expellees who came from Silesia, Pomerania and East Prussia, which had belonged to the German Reich as it had been constituted in the wake of World War I, the Lodzer could not cling to the legal fiction that they had fled or been expelled from a place that was under temporary administration by a foreign power until a peace treaty restored their homeland to Germany. The onetime German inhabitants of Lodz knew they had no claim under international law: Lodz had been part of Poland until September 1, 1939, and it was legally so after May 8, 1945. And neither the Polish government nor the Polish citizens of Lodz would ever condone a return of the Germans who, between September 1939 and January 1945, had been less than good neighbours.

It appears only one of them set out to deal with the ugly last chapter in the history of their community, when Lodzers either stood by or actively participated in the destruction of the Jewish community and the killing of more than 200,000 Jews. In 2012, a book was published by Jens-Jürgen Ventzki, the son of Werner Ventzki, who had served between early 1941 and the middle of 1943 as the Mayor of Lodz and, as such, had been the supreme ruler of the Lodz Ghetto. The book is a son's reckoning with his father's record. The younger Ventzki was born in Lodz in March 1944, and only found out about his father's role in the destruction of the Lodz Jews when, in 1990, he visited an exhibition on the Lodz Ghetto held at the Jewish Museum in Frankfurt am Main. One of the panels showed a reproduction of letter written by his father concerning the destination of clothing of Jews killed in Chełmno.

For a decade, Ventzki was unable to deal with this discovery, but in 2001 he travelled for the first time to the place of his birth. This trip was the beginning of ten years of intensive work to understand both his father (and his mother, who had also been an active Nazi) and what had happened in Lodz during his administration. In May 2011, Ventzki met students in Lodz, and spoke about his work and his past. Growing up in Bonn, where his father had become a high-ranking civil servant, he had never heard any details about his father's time in Lodz. "In the family one always said: Łódź is an ugly city, an industrial city in Poland. That settled the issue. And I couldn't boast about this in school," he explained. Yet there was one detail on which Ventzki picked up: when his father spoke about Lodz, he always used the name "Litzmannstadt." "There was no Łódź, but always only Litzmannstadt." To the son, the key question was the relation between the Lodz Ghetto and the German city of Litzmannstadt. "The synchronism, the parallelism in Łódź has always intrigued me, and continues to do so. How was it possible in Łódź, then Litzmannstadt, in such a situation and for a first time such a strong parallelism: one the one side the ghetto, and there not a few people in the ghetto. And on the other side the Germans." Ventzki recalled his father's success in getting famous artists to visit the city, the concerts and cultural events, the many modes of entertainment, "while one knew that the ghetto exists, that people are starving there, that they're ill, die, and are deported."[1]

Ventzki has tried to bring these two histories together, through study and by meeting survivors of the Lodz Ghetto such as Michael Checinski and Leon Zelman.

> I got to know [Checinski] in Vienna. We shook hands. It was difficult for him and for me too. He is now unfortunately deceased. We shook hands. He did not let go of my hand. When you shake hands, it's actually a matter of seconds. Then one lets go. But at our first meeting he held my hand for several minutes. A lot of emotions went through my head and my heart. Because I realized that it is important, and that it can not be wrong, to talk and, what is really important for our side, for the side of the perpetrators, for the side of the younger generation, to listen. To show interest, and not to bury anything in silence.[2]

By the time Ventzki met Checinski and Zelman, neither of the two ghetto survivors lived in Lodz, or Poland, for that matter. Like almost all survivors of the Lodz Ghetto, they decided, mostly sooner but sometimes also later, to rebuild their lives elsewhere. In that respect, their postwar history shows a parallel with that of the Germans, who had either fled the city or were expelled. In February 1945, some survivors established the Provisional Jewish Committee with the aim of recreating a basis for Jewish life in the city, and historian Philip Friedman established the Central Jewish Historical Commission in order to begin the enormous task of reconstructing the catastrophe. With Warsaw in ruins and Lodz largely untouched by artillery shells and bombs, many Polish Jews returning from the paradoxical refuge offered in the Soviet Union settled in Lodz, and by the middle of 1946, the Jewish community had grown from the 877 ghetto survivors who had greeted the Red Army in January 1945 to 30,000 people. These included Marek Edelman, who became after the death of Mordechaj Anielewicz the head of the Warsaw Ghetto Uprising, and who studied medicine in Lodz and became a well-known cardiologist in the city, as well as filmmaker and Lodz native Aleksander Ford (born Mosze Lifszyc), who had survived the war in the Soviet Union and was to have a crucial role in re-establishing the Polish film industry and helping to shape, as a professor at the National Film School in Lodz, the careers of Andrzej Wajda and Roman Polański.

But few Jews chose to remain: as the Iron Curtain separating Europe came down, many slipped out of the city and clandestinely crossed the Czechoslovakian and German borders, ending up displaced persons in camps in the American Zone of Occupation in Germany, awaiting new homes in the Americas, Australia or Palestine. Only a very small remnant stayed behind: the members of this group were generally committed socialists, such as Edelman, or Communists, such as Ford, who believed in the social promise of the *Polska Rzeczpospolita Ludowa* (Polish People's Republic). Most of them—including Ford and Alina Margolis-Edelman, Marek Edelman's wife—left Poland after the leadership of this once-promising state adopted anti-Zionism as a state policy in the wake of the Six-Day War. Yet Edelman, who by 1968 was the most famous citizen of Lodz, decided not to follow his wife. "Someone had to stay here with all those who perished here, after all."[3]

He had work to do: in a city in which thousands of Jewish lives had been lost, he tenaciously sought to save every last one—Jewish or non-Jewish—with a humanism born from the abyss he had faced. The Polish Jewish child-survivor and poet Hanna Krall recorded in her biographical essay on Edelman fragments of a conversation. "People have told me, Marek, that when you're taking care of simple and not terrible serious cases, you do it in a way out of a sense of duty, that you only really light up when the game begins, when the race with death begins." Edelman found this self-evident: "This is, after all, my role," he told Krall.

God is trying to blow out the candle and I'm quickly trying to shield the flame, taking advantage of His brief inattention. To keep the flame flickering, even if only for a little while longer than He would wish.

It is important: He is not terribly just. It can also be very satisfying, because whenever something does work out, it means you have, after all, fooled Him...[4]

Edelman felt justified in fooling God because, having witnessed the destruction of a community of 400,000 people in Warsaw, and having settled in a city where a community of more than 200,000 Jews had been destroyed, he had some things to settle with Him. It was a slow process, he admitted:

> There will be long days of waiting, because only gradually will it be revealed whether the heart will adapt to the patched-up veins, to the new aortas, and to the medication. Later, gradually, you get calmer, you become more confident. ... And as this tension and later this happiness gradually leaves you, only then do you finally realize the proportion: one to four hundred thousand.
>   1:400,000
>   It is simply ludicrous.
>   But every life is a full one hundred percent for each individual, so that perhaps it makes some sense after all.[5]

Today, like Poland itself, Lodz is a city with an almost exclusively ethnic Polish population. While the town had ethnic Polish roots, its rise into a metropolis was the result of immigration—of first Germans, and then Jews—and the Poles had been the last group to shape city. The establishment of the Polish state in 1918 ensured their dominance over the city, and the destruction of the Jewish community between 1939 and 1945 and the flight and expulsion of the Germans between 1944 and 1947 made them into the proverbial last men standing.

With almost all of the industry that made it great gone bankrupt, Lodz has tried, with some success, to shed its Cinderella-like reputation and reinvent itself as a major cultural destination. Yet despite the magnificent renovation of Izrael Poznański's textile mill into the Manufaktura cultural and shopping centre, Lodz remains in the shadow of Kraków, Warsaw and Gdańsk. In one of the best English-language tourist guides for the region, Rick Steves's *Eastern Europe*, Poland occupies 246 pages. Of these, Kraków takes eighty-eight pages,

Warsaw fifty, Gdańsk fifty, and Auschwitz-Birkenau no fewer than eighteen. Not a single page is devoted to Lodz. In fact, its name only appears once, in the two-page "Poland Almanac" that provides the most important facts: "Official Name: Rzeczpospolita Polska; Area: 122,000 square miles; Population: 38.5 million" and so on. "Biggest Cities: Warsaw (the capital, 1.7 million), Kraków (757,000), and Łódź (747,000)."[6] That's all the English-speaking traveller needs to know about Lodz.

As to the memory of the Lodz Ghetto: the very fact that the most famous Jew in postwar Lodz was a leader and survivor of the Warsaw Ghetto Uprising symbolically indicates that the glory of the latter will always overshadow the troubled memory of the former. And the history of the Lodz Ghetto will always been chained to the vain, megalomaniac and at the same time both ruthlessly and narrowly competent Rumkowski, to the kind of factory-society he created, and most importantly to the decision he took in September 1942 to sacrifice the children, the sick and the elderly for the sake of the continued existence of the ghetto as a place of efficient production. "That a Rumkowski should have emerged from Lodz's affliction is painful and distressing," Levi observed forty years later. "But there are extenuating circumstances: an infernal order such as National Socialism exercises a frightful power of corruption, against which it is difficult to guard oneself. It degrades its victims and makes them similar to itself, because it needs both great and small complicities. To resist it requires a truly solid moral armature, and the one available to Rumkowski, the Lodz merchant, together with his entire generation, was fragile."[7] And, as we have seen, the Lodz Ghetto was without any support from the neighbouring community.

During the Eichmann Trial, in which Ross bore witness on behalf of the Jews of Lodz, the judges repeatedly asked the survivor-witnesses if they had received any help from non-Jews. Most often, the answer was no. Yet there were exceptions. The court heard the story of a German non-commissioned officer named Anton Schmidt who had helped Jewish partisans. Hannah Arendt was in the courtroom when this story was told, and she noted that the court went totally silent. "In those two minutes, which were like a sudden burst of light in the midst of impenetrable, unfathomable darkness, a single thought stood out clearly, irrefutably, beyond question—how utterly different everything would be today in this courtroom, in Israel, in Germany, in all of Europe, and perhaps in all countries in the world, if only more such stories could have been told."[8]

Focusing on the bystanders who were not consumed by the virus of racial anti-Semitism, but who were ordinary, decent people, Arendt turned to the memoir of Curt Emmrich, a German physician who had watched, without protest, the killing of Jews in Sevastopol. This memoir had made waves in post-war Germany because of a single sentence: *"Wir wußten das. Wir taten nichts"* ("We knew it. We did nothing").[9] Writing under the pseudonym Peter Bamm, Emmrich explained in sophisticated and self-serving language that many like him might have done something if they could have died a martyr's death. Yet Nazi Germany did not provide that honour to its opponents. "The totalitarian state lets its opponents disappear in silent anonymity. It is certain that anyone who had dared to suffer death rather than silently tolerate the crime would have sacrificed his life in vain. This is not to say that such a sacrifice would have been morally meaningless. It would only have been practically useless."[10]

Arendt had no difficulty in pointing out the fallacy of Emmrich's argument. While she acknowledged that totalitarianism aims to create "holes of oblivion into which all deeds, good or evil, would disappear," she also pointed out that such holes of oblivion do not exist. "Nothing human is that perfect, and there are simply too many people in the world to make oblivion possible. One man will always be left alive to tell the story. Hence, nothing can ever be 'practically useless,' at least, not in the long run."[11] Arendt did not address the unique case of death in the gas chambers, but I believe her judgment is solid: despite the best efforts of the Nazis to make *der Jude* disappear without a trace, and despite the best efforts made by them to erase the traces of their disappearing by burning libraries and documents, levelling Jewish neighborhoods, dismantling gas chambers, emptying mass graves and scattering ashes, the Holocaust of the Jews is one of the best documented genocides in history.

This applies to the murder of six million Jews as a whole, and it applies to major aspects of that genocide, including the German creation and liquidation of the Lodz Ghetto, and the ways Jews imprisoned in that place tried to cope with the daily destitution, humiliation and violence that came their way. This, then, points to both the moral meaning and the practical use of the 3,000 negatives that Ross made between 1940 and 1944, and which in 1945 he was able to recover from the ruins of the Lodz Ghetto.

A decade ago, Thomas Weber offered me the opportunity and privilege to write a foreword to *The Łódź Ghetto Album*, the first publication of the hitherto suppressed photos taken by Henryk Ross in the Lodz Ghetto. I enjoyed this task, but also believed it to be my first and last engagement with this striking visual and historical material. A few years later, Ross's negatives were given to the Art Gallery of Ontario in Toronto. When Maia-Mari Sutnik, the AGO's Curator of Photography, Special Projects, began to think about an exhibition based on these negatives, she remembered that the writer of the aforementioned foreword lived up the road, and invited me to join the project by writing a historical introduction to the Lodz Ghetto for the book that was to accompany the show. In the months that followed, I got to work with Maia; the gallery's Manager of Publishing, Jim Shedden; Project Manager Valentine Moreno; the Editor of Publications & Exhibitions, Claire Crighton; and my fellow authors Eric Beck Rubin, Bernice Eisenstein and Michael Mitchell. When my contribution proved too long for the multi-author book, my agent Beverley Slopen suggested the AGO publish a summary of the text I had written as a chapter, and further develop the manuscript into a short book that might be published as an e-book or a book-on-demand. Bev, Maia and Jim came to an agreement, and Claire went to work with the proverbial editor's scissors and attended to the manuscript that has become the book in your hands. I thank all of you—Tom, Maia, Jim, Valentine, Claire, Eric, Bernice, Michael and Bev—for your friendship and support.

And I thank Miriam Greenbaum, who so often interrupted her own work, and immediately read and marked up every page of every version of the manuscript when it landed on her desk, who gave me general feedback, pointed criticism and, at times, much-needed encouragement.

Robert Jan van Pelt
Toronto, September 2014

PROLOGUE

1   See Jürgen Hensel, ed., *Polen, Deutsche und Juden in Lodz 1820–1939: Eine schwierige Nachbarschaft* (Osnabrück: Fibre-Verlag, 1999); Krystyna Radziszewska, ed., *Pod Jednym Dachem: Niemcy oraz ich polscy i żydowscy sąsiedzi w Łodzi w XIX i XX wieku* (Lodz: Literatura, 2000); Jörg Roesler, "Lodz—Die Industriestadt als Schmelztiegel der Ethnien? Probleme des Zusammenlebens von Polen, Juden und Deutschen im 'polnischen Manchester' (1865–1945)," *Jahrbuch für Forschungen zur Geschichte der Arbeiterbewegung*, vol. 5, issue 2 (2006), 121–129.

2   Alfred Döblin, *Reise in Polen* (Olten and Freiburg im Breisgau: Walter-Verlag, 1968), 322; Döblin, *Journey to Poland*, trans. Joachim Neugroschel (London and New York: I.B. Tauris, 1991), 247.

3   Julian Tuwim, "Łódź," in Julian Tuwim, *Dzieła*, 5 vols. (Warsaw: Czytelnik, 1955–1964), vol. 3, 142.

4   See Oskar Rosenfeld, *In the Beginning was the Ghetto: Notebooks from Łódź*, trans. Brigitte M. Goldstein (Evanston: Northwestern University Press, 2002), 38.

5   John Ruskin, *Sesame and Lilies* (New York: Silver, Burdett and Company, 1900), 27.

6   Janina Struk, *Photographing the Holocaust: Interpretations of the Evidence* (London: I.B. Taurus, 2004), 86–89.

7   Ibid., 93.

8   *The Trial of Adolf Eichmann*, Session 24, 16 Iyar, 5721 (2 May 1961), http://www.nizkor.org/hweb/people/e/eichmann-adolf/transcripts/Sessions/Session-024-01.html.

9   Henryk Ross, Łódź Ghetto Album, ed. Thomas Weber, Martin Parr and Timothy Pruss (London: Archive of Modern Conflict, 2004).

10 Guy Miron and Shlomit Shulhani, eds., *The Yad Vashem Encyclopedia of the Ghettos during the Holocaust*, 2 vols. (Jerusalem: Yad Vashem, 2009), vol. 1, xl.

11 In Hubert Müller, ed., *Der Osten des Warthelandes* (Stuttgart: Stähle & Friedel, 1941), 241–244.

12 Ibid.

CHAPTER ONE

1   On the history of the Germans in Lodz, see Stefan Dyroff, Krystyna Radziszewska and Isabel Röskau-Rydel, eds., *Lodz jenseits von Fabriken, Wildwest und Provinz: Kulturwissenschaftliche Studien über die Deutschen in und aus den polnischen Gebieten* (Munich: Martin Meidenbauer, 2009); and Andrzej Machejek, ed., *Niemcy łódzcy/Die Lodzer Deutschen* (Lodz: Wydawn, 2010).

2   On the history of the Jews in Lodz see the special volume of *Polin* devoted to Lodz:
     Anthony Polansky, ed., *Polin: A Journal of Polish-Jewish Studies*, vol. 6 (Oxford: Blackwell,
     1991). Also: Andrej Machejek, ed., *Żydzi Łodzcy/Jews of Łódź* (Lodz: Wydawnictwo
     Hamal, 2004); and Paweł Spodenkiewicz, *The Missing District: People and Places of Jewish
     Łódź*, trans. Dorota Wiśniewska and John Crust (Lodz: Wydawn, 2007).

3   Oskar Kossmann, *Lodz: Eine historisch-geographische Analyse* (Würzburg: Holzner, 1966);
     Stanisław Liszewski, "The Origins and Stages of Development of Industrial Łódź and
     of Łódź Urban Region," in *A Comparative Study of Łódź and Manchester: Geographies of
     European Cities in Transition*, ed. Stanisław Liszewski and Craig Young, (Lodz: Łódź
     University Press, 1997), 11–33.

4   See Wojciech Kallas, "New Global Mapping: The City of Lódz in Wladyslaw St. Reymont's
     The Promised Land," *Phantasma: The Center for Imagination Studies*, http://phantasma.ro/
     wp/?p=3164&lang=en.

5   Ladislas Reymont, *The Promised Land*, trans. M.H. Dziewicki, 2 vols. (London: Knopf,
     1928), vol. 1, 7.

6   Rosa Luxemburg, *Wybór Pism*, 2 vols. (Warsaw: Książka i Wiedza, 1959), vol. 2, 64–65.

7   Richard Breyer, Peter E. Nasarski and Janusz Piekalkiewicz, *Nachbarn seit tausend Jahren:
     Deutsche und Polen in Bildern und Dokumenten* (Mainz: Hase & Koehler, 1976), 209.

8   See Robert Jan van Pelt, "Freemasonry and Judaism," in *Handbook of Freemasonry*, ed.
     Henrik Bogdan and Jan A.M. Snoek (Leiden: Brill, 2014), 188–232.

9   In "Der Deutsche Verein für Lodz und Umgegend: Seine Entstehung und Entwcklung,"
     Jahrbuch des deutschen Vereins für Lodz und Umgegend, vol. 1 (1917), 7.

10   Jack Wertheimer, *Unwelcome Strangers: East European Jews in Imperial Germany* (New
     York: Oxford University Press, 1987).

11   In Sander L. Gilman, *Jewish Self-Hatred* (Baltimore: Johns Hopkins University Press,
     1986), 102.

12   David Friedländer, *Über die Verbesserung der Israeliten im Königreich Pohlen* (Berlin:
     Nicolaïschen Buchhandlung, 1819), xlvi.

13   Jakob Wasserman, *Mein Weg als Deutscher und Jude* (Berlin: S. Fischer Verlag, 1921),
     107–108.

14   Hermann Cohen, "The Polish Jew," in *The Jew: Essays from Martin Buber's Journal,
     Der Jude, 1916–1928*, ed. Arthur A. Cohen, trans. Joachim Neugroschel (Tuscaloosa,
     AL: University of Alabama Press, 1980), 58.

15   Exodus 22:21.

16   Hermann Cohen, *Religion der Vernunft aus den Quellen des Judentums* (Leipzig: Gustav
     Fock, 1919), 141.

17   Oskar Singer, *"Im Eilschritt durch den Gettotag..."*: *Reportagen und Essays aus dem Getto
     Lodz*, ed. Sascha Feuchert et al. (Berlin and Vienna, Philo, 2002), 180–181.

18   Tuwim, "Wspomnienia o Łodzi," *Dzieła*, vol. 5, 40–41.

19 In Andreas Kossert, "'Promised Land'? Urban Myth and the Shaping of Modernity in Manchester and Lodz," in *Imagining the City*, ed. Christian Emden, Catherine Keen and David Midgley, 2 vols. (Oxford and New York: Peter Lang, 2006), vol. 2, 178.

20 Döblin, *Journey to Poland*, 231–232, 243–244.

21 Ibid.

22 Ibid., 234–235.

23 Karl Weber, *Litzmannstadt: Geschichte und Probleme eines Wirtschaftszentrums im deutschen Osten* (Jena: Gustav Fischer, 1943), 8–10.

CHAPTER TWO

1   Alfred Rosenberg, "Die Protokolle der Weisen von Zion und die jüdische Weltpolitik," in *Schriften und Reden*, 2 vols. (Munich: Hoheneichen-Verlag, 1943), vol. 2, 428.

2   Thomas Weber, *Hitler's First War: Adolf Hitler, the Men of the List Regiment, and the First World War* (New York: Oxford University Press, 2011).

3   Adolf Hitler, *Mein Kampf*, trans. Ralph Manheim (Boston: Houghton Mifflin, 1943), 52, 56–57.

4   My argument on the critical importance of making *der Jude* visible is inspired and guided by Dan Michman's reflections on this topic. See Dan Michman, "The Jewish Dimension of the Holocaust in Dire Straits?: Current Challenges of Interpretation and Scope," in *Jewish Histories of the Holocaust: New Transnational Approaches*, ed. Norman J. W. Goda (New York and Oxford: Berghahn, 2014), 17–38, especially 23–26.

5   Kossmann, *Lodz*, 146–147.

6   Ibid., 145–147.

7   Tuwim, "Anonimowe Mocarstwo," *Dzieła*, vol. 3, 50.

8   Peter-Heinz Seraphim, *Polen und seine Wirtschaft* (Königsberg: Institut für Osteuropäische Wirtschaft, 1937), 20–21, plate 36.

9   On the importance of Seraphim's book in the history of the Holocaust, see Michman, *The Emergence of the Jewish Ghettos during the Holocaust*, trans. Lenn J. Schramm (New York: Cambridge University Press, 2011). In 1937, Seraphim published an early discussion on his idea of the ghetto as "Das ostjüdische Ghetto," in *Jomsburg: Völker und Staaten im Osten und Norden Europas*, vol. 1 (1937), 439–465.

10 Peter-Heinz Seraphim, *Das Judentum im osteuropäischen Raum* (Essen: Essener Verlagsanstalt, 1938), 358, 362, 365, 371.

11 Ibid., 371.

12 Ibid., 658, 673.

13 See Cornelia Schmitz-Berning, *Vokabular des Nationalsozialismus* (Berlin and New York: Walter de Gruyter: 1998), 686–689. Also: Emil Fackenheim, "Holocaust and *Weltanschauung*: Philosophical Reflections on Why They Did It," *Holocaust and Genocide Studies*, vol. 3 (1988), 204.

14 "Stenographic Report of the Meeting on the Jewish Question held under the Chairmanship of Field Marshal Goering in the Reich Air Ministry at 11 A.M. on November 12," in Yithzak Arad, Israel Gutman and Abraham Margaliot, *Documents on the Holocaust: Selected Sources on the Destruction of the Jews of Germany and Austria, Poland and the Soviet Union*, trans. Lea Ben-Dor (Lincoln: University of Nebraska Press, 1999), 110–111.

15 Hans Meyerhof, "Refugees and 'Ejectees,'" *Jewish Frontier*, vol. 7 (April 1941), 7.

16 Martin Gumpert, *First Papers*, trans. Heinz Norden and Ruth Norden (New York: Duell, Sloan and Pearce, 1941), 30.

17 Joseph Roth, *The Wandering Jews*, trans. Michael Hofmann (New York and London: Norton, 2001), 1–5.

18 Joseph Roth, "Preface to the New Edition (1937)," *The Wandering Jews*, 122–123.

19 Stefan Zweig, *The World of Yesterday* (London: Cassell, 1943), 319–320.

CHAPTER THREE

1 Peter-Heinz Seraphim, *Ostdeutschland und das heutige Polen* (Brunswick: Georg Westermann Verlag, 1953), plate 10.

2 Walter Christaller, Die Zentralen Orte in den Ostgebieten und ihre Kultur- und Marktbereiche (Leipzig: K. F. Koehler Verlag, 1941), 20–21.

3 The concept of the Wartheland as a blond province to be was coined by Himmler during a visit to Posen in December 1939. See: Catherine Epstein, *Model Nazi: Arthur Greiser and the Occupation of Western Poland* (Oxford: Oxford University Press, 2010), 161.

4 Robert Lewis Koehl, *RKFDV: German Resettlement and Population Policy, 1939–1945. A History of the Reich Commission for the Strengthening of Germandom* (Cambridge: Harvard University Press, 1957).

5 In Raphael Gross and Werner Renz, eds., *Der Frankfurter Auschwitz-Prozess (1963–1965): Kommentierte Quellenedition*, 2 vols. (Frankfurt and New York, Campus, 2013), vol. 1, 177.

6 The standard work on the persecution and Holocaust of the Jews in the Wartheland is Michael Alberti, *Die Vervolgung und Vernichtung der Juden im Reichsgau Wartheland, 1939–1945* (Wiesbaden: Harrassowitz Verlag, 2006).

7 See *Der deutsche Wochenschau*, no. 472 (September 20, 1939).

8 Joseph Goebbels, *Die Tägebücher von Joseph Goebbels: Teil I*, ed. Elke Fröhlich, 14 vols. to date (Munich: K.G. Saur, 1998–ongoing), vol. 7, 157, 173, 177, 179–180.

9 Laurence Rees, "The Most Appalling Film in History," ww2history.com/blog/ww2—anniversary/the-most-appalling-film-in-history/.

10 *Der Ewige Jude*, film, dir. Fritz Hippler (Berlin: Deutsche Filmherstellungs-und-Verwertungs-GmbH, 1940).

11 Ibid.

12 Ibid.

13 Heinz Schwaibold, "Wie der Film 'Der ewige Jude' enstand," *Kreiszeitung für Ost-Prignitz*, December 4, 1940, in *Die Verfolgung und Ermordung der europäischen Juden durch das nationalsozialistische Deutschland 1933–1945: Band 3, Deutsches Reich und Protektorat Böhmen un Mähren, September 1939–September 1941*, ed. Andrea Löw (Munich: Oldenburg Verlag, 2012), 334.

14 Heinz Boberach, ed., *Meldungen aus dem Reich, 1938–1945: Die geheime Lageberichte des Sicherheitsdienstes der SS*, 17 vols. (Herrsching: Pawlak, 1984), vol. 6, 1918.

15 Everett Cherrington Hughes, *On Work, Race, and the Sociological Imagination* (Chicago: University of Chicago Press, 1994), 183.

16 See Isaiah Trunk, *Łódź Ghetto: A History*, trans. Robert Moses Shapiro (Bloomington and Indianapolis, Indiana University Press, 2006).

17 In Epstein, *Model Nazi*, 167.

18 Jonny Moser, *Nisko: Die ersten Judendeportationen*, ed. Joseph W. Moser and James R. Moser (Vienna: Edition Steinbauer, 2012).

19 In Gross and Renz, eds., *Der Frankfurter Auschwitz-Prozess (1963–1965)*, vol. 1, 177–178.

20 Michman, "The Jewish Ghettos under the Nazis and Their Allies: The Reasons behind Their Emergence," in *The Yad Vashem Encyclopedia of the Ghettos during the Holocaust*, ed. Miron and Shulhani, vol. 1, xxi, xxiii. See also: Michman, *The Emergence of Jewish Ghettos During the Holocaust* (Cambridge: Cambridge University Press, 2011).

CHAPTER FOUR

1 In Trunk, *Łódź Ghetto*, 20.

2 Ibid., 21.

3 Kossmann, *Lodz*, 108.

4 Sholem Aleichem, *The Old Country: Collected Stories of Sholom Aleichem* (New York: Crown Publishers, 1946), 7.

5 In Trunk, *Łódź Ghetto*, 24.

6 *Lodscher Zeitung*, February 11, 1940, in Michman, *The Emergence of Jewish Ghettos During the Holocaust*, 81.

7 A useful primer on the history of the Lodz Ghetto is Julian Baranowski, *The Łódź Ghetto, 1940–1944/Łódzkie Getto, 1940–1944: Vademecum* (Lodz: Archiwum Państwowe w Łodzi/Bilbo, 1999). An important interpretation of the history of the Lodz Ghetto in the context of the Germanization of the city is offered in Gordon J. Horwitz, *Ghettostadt: Łódź and the Making of a Nazi City* (Cambridge, MA: Harvard University Press, 2008).

8 Karl Weber, "Die deutsche Wirtschaft in Lodsch: Ihre Entstehung, Entwicklung und ihr Kampf zu polnischer Zeit," *Warthegau-Wirtschaft: Organ der Wirtschaftskammer Warthegau*, vol. 1, no. 1 (February 1940), 6–7.

9 In Epstein, *Model Nazi*, 1769–1970.

10 In Michman, *The Emergence of Jewish Ghettos During the Holocaust*, 82.

11 Hubert Müller, ed., *Der Osten des Warthelandes* (Stuttgart: Stähle & Friedel, 1941), 11.

12 Ibid., 11, 241–244.

13 In Trunk, Łódź Ghetto, 31.
14 "Die Juden in Litzmannstatd," Frankfurter Zeitung, May 19, 1940, in Jens-Jürgen Ventzki, Seine Schatten, meine Bilder: Eine Spurensuche (Innsbruck: Studienverlag, 2011), 44.
15 Ibid., 64.
16 See Samuel D. Kassow, Who Will Write Our History?: Emanuel Ringelblum, the Warsaw Ghetto, and the Oyneg Shabes Archive (Bloomington and Indianapolis: Indiana University Press, 2007), 92–93.
17 Litzmannstadt (Litzmannstadt: Seipelt, 1941).
18 Herman Melville, Moby Dick, ed. Harrison Hayford and Hershel Parker (New York: Norton, 1967), 163–164, 169.
19 Karl Weber, "Von Lodsch zu Litzmannstadt," Warthegau-Wirtschaft: Organ der Wirtschaftskammer Warthegau, vol. 1, no. 5 (June 1940), 4–5.
20 Karl Marder, "Litzmannstadt: Eine deutsche Schöpfung und eine deutsche Aufgabe," Warthegau-Wirtschaft: Organ der Wirtschaftskammer Warthegau, vol. 1, no. 5 (June 1940), 2–3.
21 Tuwim, "Anonimowe Mocarstwo," Dzieła, vol. 3, 50.

CHAPTER FIVE

1 Reinhard Heydrich to Joachim von Ribbentrop, June 24, 1940, in Die Verfolgung und Ermordung der europäischen Juden durch das nationalsozialistische Deutschland 1933–1945: Band 3, Deutsches Reich und Protektorat Böhmen un Mähren, September 1939–September 1941, ed. Andrea Löw (Munich: Oldenburg Verlag, 2012), 247.
2 Minutes of meeting between Greiser, Frank and others held in Kraków on July 31, 1940, in Die Verfolgung und Ermordung der europäischen Juden durch das nationalsozialistische Deutschland 1933–1945: Band 4, Polen, September 1939–September 1941, ed. Klaus-Peter Friedrich with Andrea Löw (Munich: Oldenburg Verlag, 2011), 342.
3 Alberti, Die Verfolgung und Vernichtung der Juden im Reichsgau Wartheland, 158–159.
4 In Christopher Browning with Jürgen Matthäus, The Origins of the Final Solution: The Evolution of Nazi Jewish Policy, September 1939–March 1942 (Lincoln and Jerusalem: University of Nebraska Press and Yad Vashem, 2004), 119–120.
5 Alberti, Die Verfolgung und Vernichtung der Juden im Reichsgau Wartheland, 251.
6 Primo Levi, The Drowned and the Saved, trans. Raymond Rosenthal (New York: Summit Books, 1986), 43
7 In Alberti, Die Verfolgung und Vernichtung der Juden im Reichsgau Wartheland, 265.
8 Daily Chronicle of the Litzmannstadt Ghetto, February 8, 1941, in Die Verfolgung und Ermordung der europäischen Juden durch das nationalsozialistische Deutschland 1933–1945: Band 4, 523–524.
9 In Alberti, Die Verfolgung und Vernichtung der Juden im Reichsgau Wartheland, 267.
10 Shlomo Frank, diary entry of January 30, 1941, in Die Verfolgung und Ermordung der europäischen Juden durch das nationalsozialistische Deutschland 1933–1945: Band 4, 514.

11 In Alexandra Zapruder, *Salvaged Pages: Young Writers' Diaries of the Holocaust* (New Haven and London: Yale University Press, 2002), 238.

12 *The Trial of Adolf Eichmann*, Session 23, 6 Iyar, 5721 (2 May 1961), http://www.nizkor.org/ hweb/people/e/eichmann-adolf/transcripts/Sessions/Session-023-05.html.

13 Singer, *"Im Eilschritt durch den Gettotag . . ."*, 81, 87.

14 Rainer Maria Rilke, *Selected Poems*, trans. Albert Ernest Fleming (New York and Toronto: Methuen, 1986), 56.

15 Hannah Arendt, "The Concentration Camps," *Partisan Review*, vol. 15, no. 7 (July 1948), 756.

CHAPTER SIX

1 See Henry Friedländer, *The Origins of Nazi Genocide: From Euthanasia to the Final Solution* (Chapel Hill and London: University of North Carolina Press, 1995); and Christopher R. Browning with Jürgen Matthäus, *The Origins of the Final Solution: The Evolution of Nazi Jewish Policy, September 1939–March 1942* (Lincoln and Jerusalem: University of Nebraska Press and Yad Vashem, 2004).

2 Rolf-Heinz Höppner to Adolf Eichmann, July 16, 1941, in Friedrich with Löw, eds., *Die Verfolgung und Ermordung der europäischen Juden durch das nationalsozialistische Deutschland 1933–1945: Band 4*, 680–681.

3 Lucjan Dobroszycki, ed., *The Chronicle of the Łódź Ghetto, 1941–1945*, trans. Richard Lourie, Joachim Neugorschel et al. (New Haven and London: Yale University Press, 1984), 83.

4 Singer, "Im Eilschritt durch den Gettotag...", 187–189.

5 Ibid.,187.

6 Rosenfeld, *In the Beginning was the Ghetto*, 15.

7 Dobroszycki, ed., *The Chronicle of the Łódź Ghetto*, 112.

8 Singer, *"Im Eilschritt durch den Gettotag..."*, 188–189.

9 William Shakespeare, *The Tempest* 2.2.44.

10 Alfred Döblin, "Eindrücke von New York," *Schriften zu Leben und Werk* (Olten and Freiburg: Walter-Verlag, 1986), 245–246.

11 Alfred Döblin, *Destiny's Journey*, trans. Edna McCown (New York: Paragon House, 1992), 193.

12 Theodor Wolff, *"Die Juden": Ein Dokument aus dem Exil, 1942/43*, ed. Bernd Sösemann (Königstein: Jüdischer Verlag Athenäum, 1984), 45.

13 Ibid., 50–51.

14 Ibid., 52.

15 Rosenfeld, *In the Beginning was the Ghetto*, 37–38.

1   See Patrick Montague, *Chelmno and the Holocaust: The History of Hitler's First Death Camp* (Chapel Hill: University of North Carolina Press, 2012).

2   Joseph Goebbels, *Die Tagebücher von Joseph Goebbels: Teil II*, ed. Elke Fröhlich, 15 vols. (Munich: Saur, 1996), vol. 2., 498–499.

3   Dobroszycki, ed., *The Chronicle of the Łódź Ghetto*, 96–97.

4   In Dobroszycki, ed., *The Chronicle of the Łódź Ghetto*, 111–112.

5   Dobroszycki, ed., *The Chronicle of the Łódź Ghetto*, 145.

6   Rosenfeld, *In the Beginning Was the Ghetto*, 104–106.

7   Dobroszycki, ed., *The Chronicle of the Łódź Ghetto*, 165–167.

8   Serge Klarsfeld, *Vichy-Auschwitz: Die "Endlösung der Judenfrage" in Frankreich* (Darmstadt: Wissenschaftliche Buchgesellschaft, 2007), 78–81, 410–411.

9   Jorge Semprun, "Une petite lampe s'est allumée dans la baraque des contagieux....," in *Élie Wiesel en Hommage* ed. Ariana Kalfa and de Michaël Saint Cheron (Paris: Les Editions du Cerf, 1998), 60–61, in Caroline Fournet, *The Crime of Destruction and the Law of Genocide: Their Impact on Collective Memory* (Aldershot: Ashgate, 2007), 32.

10 Dobroszycki, ed., *The Chronicle of the Łódź Ghetto*, 245.

11 In Alan Adelson and Robert Lapides, eds., *Łódź Ghetto: Inside a Community Under Siege* (New York: Viking, 1989), 322.

12 Ibid., *Łódź Ghetto*, 328–330.

13 Ibid., *Łódź Ghetto*, 336–338.

14 *The Trial of Adolf Eichmann*, Session 23, 6 Iyar, 5721 (2 May 1961), http://www.nizkor.org/hweb/people/e/eichmann-adolf/transcripts/Sessions/Session-023-05.html.

15 Dobroszycki, ed., *The Chronicle of the Łódź Ghetto*, 254–255.

16 Rosenfeld, *In the Beginning was the Ghetto*, 176.

17 Franz Rosenzweig, *The Star of Redemption*, trans. William H. Hallow (London: Routledge & Kegan Paul, 1971), 298.

18 Dobroszycki, ed., *The Chronicle of the Łódź Ghetto*, 258.

19 Frank Stier, *Kriegsauftrag 160: Behelfsheimbau im Ghetto Litzmannstadt (Łódź) und im KZ-Aussenlager Königs Wusterhausen durch das Deutsche Wohnungshilfswerk* (Berlin: Arenhövel, 1999).

CHAPTER EIGHT

1   In Zapruder, *Salvaged Pages*, 371.
2   Ibid., 372.
3   Dobroszycki, ed., *The Chronicle of the Łódź Ghetto*, 514.
4   Ibid., 526.
5   In Zapruder, *Salvaged Pages*, 374.
6   Ibid., 376–377.
7   Rosenfeld, *In the Beginning was the Ghetto*, 280–281.
8   In Adelson and Lapides, eds., Łódź Ghetto, 440.
9   Ibid., 441.
10   In Zapruder, *Salvaged Pages*, 393–394.
11   Frank Stier, *Kriegsauftrag*, 160.

EPILOGUE

1   "Jens-Jürgen Ventzki: Transkription der Begegnung mit Studenten, Dozenten und
     Zeitzeugen am 24.5.2011 in Germanistischen Institute der Universität Łódź" (Berlin:
     Europäischer Verein für Ost-West-Annäherung, 2011), 7. See: http://www.eva-verein.de/
     lodzer/dokumentation-lodzermenschen/BEGEGNUNG-Jens-Juergen-Ventzki.pdf.
2   Ibid., 10–13.
3   "Obituary: Marek Edelman," *The Daily Telegraph*, October 4, 2009.
4   Hanna Krall, *The Subtenant/To Outwit God*, trans. Jaroslav Anders, Joanna Stasinska
     Weschler and Lawrence Weschler (Evanston: Northwestern University Press, 1992), 215.
5   Ibid., 247.
6   Rick Steves, Cameron Hewitt et al., *Rick Steves' Eastern Europe* (Berkeley: Avalon Travel,
     2012), 256.
7   Levi, *The Drowned and the Saved*, 68.
8   Hannah Arendt, *Eichmann in Jerusalem: A Report on the Banality of Evil* (New York: Viking,
     1963), 210–211.
9   Peter Bamm, *Die Unsichtbare Flagge: Ein Bericht* (Munich: Kösel, 1952), 152.
10   In Arendt, *Eichmann in Jerusalem*, 211.
11   Arendt, *Eichmann in Jerusalem*, 211–212.

LEAD SUPPORTER

The Cyril & Dorothy,
Joel & Jill Reitman Family Foundation

GENEROUSLY SUPPORTED BY

A friend in Ottawa, in memory of the perished

Jack Weinbaum Family Foundation
Gerald Sheff & Shanitha Kachan
MDC Partners—Miles S. Nadal
Gerald Schwartz & Heather Reisman
Marion & Gerald Soloway
Ed & Fran Sonshine
Larry & Judy Tanenbaum & family

Apotex Foundation—Honey & Barry Sherman
Daniel Bjarnason & Nance Gelber
D. H. Gales Family Foundation
Wendy & Elliott Eisen
Saul & Toby Feldberg
Beatrice Fischer
Joe & Budgie Frieberg
Lillian & Norman Glowinsky
Maxine Granovsky Gluskin & Ira Gluskin
The Jay and Barbara Hennick Family Foundation
Warren & Debbie Kimel
The Koschitzky Family
Steven & Lynda Latner
In memory of Miriam Lindenberg by her children,
Nathan Lindenberg & Bruria Cooperman & families
Mary & Fred Litwin
Earl Rotman & Ariella Rohringer
Penny Rubinoff
Samuel & Esther Sarick
Dorothy Cohen Shoichet
Fred & Linda Waks, Jay & Deborah Waks
Anonymous

SIGNATURE PARTNER OF THE
AGO'S PHOTOGRAPHY COLLECTION PROGRAM

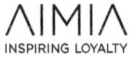

The Art Gallery of Ontario is partially funded by the Ontario Ministry of Culture. Additional operating support is received from the Volunteers of the Art Gallery of Ontario, the City of Toronto, the Department of Canadian Heritage and the Canada Council for the Arts.

Printed in Canada

10 9 8 7 6 5 4 3 2 1

This book is published in conjunction with the exhibition *Memory Unearthed: The Lodz Ghetto Photographs of Henryk Ross* Art Gallery of Ontario January 31–June 14, 2015 Curated by Maia-Mari Sutnik

Contemporary programming at the Art Gallery of Ontario is supported by

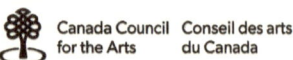

Canada Council   Conseil des arts
for the Arts   du Canada

Art Gallery of Ontario
317 Dundas Street West
Toronto, Ontario
M5T 1G4 Canada
www.ago.net

Library and Archives Canada Cataloguing in Publication

Van Pelt, Robert Jan, author

   Lodz and Getto Litzmannstadt : promised land and croaking hole of Europe / Robert Jan van Pelt.

Includes bibliographical references.
ISBN 978-1-894243-80-3 (PBK.)

   1. Litzmannstadt-Getto (Lodz, Poland). 2. Holocaust, Jewish (1939–1945)—Poland—Lodz. 3. Jews—Persecutions—Poland—Lodz—History—20th century. 4. Lodz (Poland)—History—20th century. I. Art Gallery of Ontario, issuing body II. Title.

DS134.62.V352015   940.53'1853847
C2014-906908-1

Publication

EDITOR
Claire Crighton

MANAGING EDITOR
Jim Shedden

DESIGN
Lauren Wickware

PRODUCTION ASSISTANTS
Ebony Jansen
Robyn Lew